The Rosary

Word for Word

The *Rosary*

Word for Word

A COMPANION BOOKLET

A Pearls and Beads Production

To order additional copies of this book, contact:
Xlibris
1-888-795-4274
www.Xlibris.com
Orders@Xlibris.com
665649

CONTENTS

How to Pray the Rosary

Hail Mary
< Hail Mary
< Hail Mary
< Hail Mary
< Hail Mary
< Hail Mary
< Hail Mary
< Hail Mary

Glory Be & O My Jesus >
FOURTH MYSTERY
Our Father >

Hail Mary >
Hail Mary >
Hail Mary >
Hail Mary >
Hail Mary >
Hail Mary >
Hail Mary >

Hail Mary >
Hail Mary >
Hail Mary >

Glory Be & O My Jesus >
FIFTH MYSTERY >
Our Father >
Hail Mary >
Hail Mary >
Hail Mary >
Hail Mary >
Hail Mary >
Hail Mary >
Hail Mary >
Hail Mary >
Hail Mary >
Hail Mary >

< Our Father
< THIRD MYSTERY
< Glory Be & O My Jesus
< Hail Mary
< Hail Mary
< Hail Mary
< Hail Mary
< Hail Mary
< Hail Mary
< Hail Mary
< Hail Mary
< Hail Mary
< Our Father
< SECOND MYSTERY
< Glory Be & O My Jesus
< Hail Mary
< Hail Mary
< Hail Mary
< Hail Mary
< Hail Mary
< Hail Mary
< Hail Mary
< Hail Mary
< Hail Mary

< Our Father
< FIRST MYSTERY
< Glory Be & O My Jesus
< Hail Mary
< Hail Mary
< Hail Mary
< Our Father

END HERE
at the Medallion

Hail Holy Queen

Prayer Concluding
the Rosary

Prayer to
St. Michael

Sign of the Cross

< Apostle's Creed
< Petition
< Sign of the Cross

BEGIN HERE
at the Crucifix

From Latin *Rosarium,* Meaning:
"Crown of Roses" or "Garland of Roses"

The true purpose of the Rosary is to help keep in memory certain principle events in the history of our salvation, well known as Mysteries, thanking and praising God for them. Altogether there are, twenty Mysteries reflected upon in the Rosary. They are divided into five segments.

The sequence of prayers is the Lord's Prayer, the Hail Mary ten times, the Glory Be, followed by the Fatima Prayer. Each sequence is known as a decade. Five decades are prayed, after beginning with the Apostles Creed and five initial prayers. The praying of each decade is accompanied by meditation on one of the Mysteries of the Rosary, which recall the life of Jesus.

The Rosary Meditation, Effects of Changes
In Your Life, Family & Friends

So many graces come to each of us through the recitation of the Rosary. May we all be examples, doing our part and continue each day, reciting the Rosary, to bring peace to the world.

Each Mystery meditated upon, is the soul of the Rosary. The Mysteries give life, purpose and power to the Rosary, which is so much more, than just reciting the prayer by memory. By uniting both mental and vocal prayer, it becomes one of the most beneficial ways to pray.

Sustaining a reverence and love relationship, with our Creator, through contemplating on these Mysteries, bringing graces to your own life and that of your family and friends. Praying the Rosary for yourself, each other, and the world at large, will bring harmony through the rhythm of the words, uniting our lives with the perfect lives of Jesus and His Mother, Mary.

Will we ever truly understand the effects of prayer? Or the plan of the Master's salvation through us? How He can give strength to the weak, food and shelter to the poor, bring healing to the sick, joy to the sorrowful and redemption to those who have fallen away? His ways are not our ways. Manifestations come from Him and should be recognized with appreciation. By praying the Rosary, we show love and appreciation to God our Heavenly Father, through His Son, Jesus Christ, born of the Blessed Virgin Mary.

Sometimes even our righteous ways get unraveled, bringing chaos to our lives. Daily meditating on the Rosary, gives inner strength, healing and guidance, as we journey through our labors, trials and endeavors. A prayer so powerful that even if our minds wander, we fall asleep or are involved in daily duties, the Rosary is mysteriously uniting salvation to our Redeemer for the purpose of redemption.

This is an open invitation, a call, to everyone in the world, no matter what race, religion or creed you are, to take the "Rosary Challenge". Pray the Rosary everyday because our Lord asks us to and His actions with works of love are so mysterious. The Rosary a timeless and mystical prayer. By meditating upon it, we answer His simple request.

May we be instruments of prayer like many religious and laypeople, including Saint Pope John Paul II and Blessed Mother Teresa of Calcutta, who have been walking examples, finding inner courage, strength, forgiveness and charity through the contemplation of the Rosary and their love of the Lord.

Outlined in this Booklet, are the complete prayers, word for word, to help you on your way. By using this guide you will eventually be getting yourself some Rosary beads or just keep track on your fingers, because you will have a true understanding of the pattern of the Rosary prayer. Join in this life-giving prayer to transform your life along with your family, friends, communities and the whole world.

May God bless you abundantly with the petitions of your heart for you and your loved ones, giving you graces and mercy throughout your life!

Rosary beads are one of the most beloved tools in the Catholic Church, but not limited only to Catholics. Said to have been handed down by the Blessed Virgin Mary, herself, in an apparition to St. Dominic, in 1208, in the chapel in Prouille, France. The importance of the Rosary was revisited in apparitions to Blessed Alan de la Roche, in 1460, then the three children of Fatima, in 1917. The Rosary is a promise of the Mother of God, Mary, to help those in need.

The beauty of the prayer is also represented by the unlimited loveliness in the types of beads, stones, gemstones and crucifixes that have been used to make the Rosaries throughout the world. The Rosary, itself, is not usually worn unless it is a statement of faith, usually draped on the belt of clergy, but should not be included as decorative jewelry.

The practice of meditation of the Rosary, is to focus on the life of Jesus. Novenas are said in nine days, for a particular petition in the prayer. Including, but not limited to, an end to abortion.

The Rosary is a Catholic veneration of Mary. However, Our Lady calls upon everyone in the world to join in recitation of the Holy Rosary. The Rosary beads are a way of keeping track of the prayer. There is a total of 53 Hail Mary's recited throughout each Rosary, three in the opening and 10 in each decade. There are four Rosaries, namely, the Joyful, Luminous, Sorrowful and Glorious. Each Rosary has five Mysteries to meditate upon.

We all know the power of prayer. The Holy Rosary is no exception! Memorizing and knowing the Rosary is a great thing. This companion book is a guide to get you on your way of memorization. It's a true companion for all people no matter what their belief.

The Mysteries of the Rosary are at the beginning of each decade, representative of the major events of the life of Christ, to be meditated upon during the recitation of the ten Hail Mary's.

So many times we want to say the Rosary, but unless we have all of the prayers memorized, we are not able to recite the Rosary, word for word. The context of this book allows us to focus our prayers on any of the four types of Rosaries.

Jesus is the most famous and most important person that has ever walked the face of this earth. He is true God and true man.

This book is an invitation, available and open to anyone, from any walk of life, to be shared and recited by all. Join in the Rosary meditation with your prayer requests:

"How To Pray The Rosary Effectively"

One must keep in mind, several important points, when praying the Rosary:

*Asking for favors from God through the Rosary, or prayers in general, having confidence and faith, that the prayers will not only be heard, but answered, is essential. Then allowing the solution to naturally unfold to you.

*Proven most effective, is saying the Rosary with perseverance. No matter how bleak the situation may look at times, persistently continue in your Rosary. Keep a sense of knowing the answer will come and be open to the answer.

*Make an effort to correct faults in your life. You may even make that the first intention. When praying the Rosary, you should be striving to live a generally good life.

*God as a good Father, will not always answer ones intentions, in the way one has asked. Sometimes He will not give us the intention we request, but the Rosaries are never wasted. He will use them in a different way.

*In regards to intentions for loved ones to be delivered from life choices or situations that may be harming them. We can trust with great confidence to know God wants what we want even more than

we do. Ecclesiastes 3:1, "There is an appointed time for everything. And there is a time for every event under heaven."

*The 54-Day Rosary Novena, given to us by Our Lady herself, is the best way to obtain favor. Consisting of one Rosary (5 decades) a day for 27 days in petition, followed by a Rosary in thanksgiving for another 27 days.

*Discouragement is the trap of the enemy. Don't fall into it. Almighty Father God through the Immaculate Heart of Mary will come through for you.

The Steps of the Rosary

1. *Open by making the Sign of the Cross.*

2. *Say the "Prayer Before the Rosary", (Here mention your petition).*

3. *Say the "Apostles' Creed".*

4. *Say the "Our Father".*

5. *Say three "Hail Mary's".*

6. *Say the "Glory Be" & "O My Jesus".*

7. *Announce the First Mystery.*

8. *Spiritual Fruit, Scripture, then say the "Our Father".*

9. *Say ten "Hail Mary's" while meditating on the Mystery.*

10. *Say the "Glory Be" & "O My Jesus".*

11. *Announce the Second Mystery. Repeat steps 8, 9 & 10, then continue with the Third, Fourth and Fifth Mysteries in the same manner.*

12. *Say the "Hail Holy Queen".*

13. *Say the "Concluding Rosary Prayer".*

14. *Say the "Prayer to St. Michael".*

15. *Say the "To Our Lady of Fatima Prayer".*

16. *Make the Sign of the Cross.*

Pray for World Peace!

Let us begin...

The Joyful Mysteries

In the name of the Father, and of the Son, and of the Holy Spirit. Amen.

Queen of the Holy Rosary, you have deigned to come to Fatima to reveal to the three shepherd children the treasures of Grace hidden in the Rosary. Inspire my heart with a sincere love of this devotion, in order that by meditating on the Mysteries of our Redemption which are recalled in it, I may be enriched with its fruits and obtain peace for the world, the conversion of sinners and of Russia, and the favour which I ask of you in this Rosary.

(Here mention your petition)

I ask for this for the greater glory of God, for Thine own honour, and for the good of souls, especially for my own. Amen.

I offer this Rosary for the purpose of knowing the Truth and obtaining contrition and pardon for my sins. Amen.

I believe in God, the Father Almighty, Creator of heaven and earth, and in Jesus Christ, His only Son, our Lord, who was conceived by the Holy Spirit, born of the Virgin Mary, suffered under Pontius Pilate, was crucified, died and was buried; He descended into hell; on the third day He rose again from the dead; He ascended into heaven, and is seated at the right hand of God the Father Almighty; from there He will come

to judge the living and the dead. I believe in the Holy Spirit, the Holy Catholic Church, the communion of saints, the forgiveness of sins, the resurrection of the body and life everlasting. Amen.

Our Father, Who art in heaven, Hallowed be Thy name; Thy kingdom come; Thy will be done on earth as it is in heaven. Give us this day our daily bread; and forgive us our trespasses as we forgive those who trespass against us; and lead us not into temptation, but deliver us from evil. Amen.

I.   Hail Mary, full of Grace, the Lord is with thee. Blessed art thou among women, and blessed is the fruit of thy womb, Jesus. Holy Mary, Mother of God, pray for us sinners, now and at the hour of our death. Amen.

II.   Hail Mary, full of Grace, the Lord is with thee. Blessed art thou among women, and blessed is the fruit of thy womb, Jesus. Holy Mary, Mother of God, pray for us sinners, now and at the hour of our death. Amen.

III.   Hail Mary, full of Grace, the Lord is with thee. Blessed art thou among women, and blessed is the fruit of thy womb, Jesus. Holy Mary, Mother of God, pray for us sinners, now and at the hour of our death. Amen.

Glory be to the Father, and to the Son, and to the Holy Spirit. As it was in the beginning, is now, and ever shall be, world without end. Amen.

O my Jesus, forgive us our sins, save us from the fires of hell, lead all souls to heaven, especially those in most need of Thy mercy. Amen.

The First Joyful Mystery:
"The Annunciation of the Lord"

(Spiritual Fruit: Humility)

In the sixth month, the angel Gabriel was sent from God to a town of Galilee named Nazareth, to a virgin betrothed to a man named Joseph, of the house of David. The virgin's name was Mary. (Luke 1:26-27)

Our Father, Who art in heaven, Hallowed be Thy name; Thy kingdom come; Thy will be done on earth as it is in heaven. Give us this day our daily bread; and forgive us our trespasses as we forgive those who trespass against us; and lead us not into temptation, but deliver us from evil. Amen.

I.   Hail Mary, full of Grace, the Lord is with thee. Blessed art thou among women, and blessed is the fruit of thy womb, Jesus. Holy Mary, Mother of God, pray for us sinners, now and at the hour of our death. Amen.

II.   Hail Mary, full of Grace, the Lord is with thee. Blessed art thou among women, and blessed is the fruit of thy womb, Jesus. Holy Mary, Mother of God, pray for us sinners, now and at the hour of our death. Amen.

III. Hail Mary, full of Grace, the Lord is with thee. Blessed art thou among women, and blessed is the fruit of thy womb, Jesus. Holy Mary, Mother of God, pray for us sinners, now and at the hour of our death. Amen.

IV.   Hail Mary, full of Grace, the Lord is with thee. Blessed art thou among women, and blessed is the fruit of thy womb, Jesus. Holy Mary, Mother of God, pray for us sinners, now and at the hour of our death. Amen.

V. Hail Mary, full of Grace, the Lord is with thee. Blessed art thou among women, and blessed is the fruit of thy womb, Jesus. Holy Mary, Mother of God, pray for us sinners, now and at the hour of our death. Amen.

VI. Hail Mary, full of Grace, the Lord is with thee. Blessed art thou among women, and blessed is the fruit of thy womb, Jesus. Holy Mary, Mother of God, pray for us sinners, now and at the hour of our death. Amen.

VII. Hail Mary, full of Grace, the Lord is with thee. Blessed art thou among women, and blessed is the fruit of thy womb, Jesus. Holy Mary, Mother of God, pray for us sinners, now and at the hour of our death. Amen.

VIII. Hail Mary, full of Grace, the Lord is with thee. Blessed art thou among women, and blessed is the fruit of thy womb, Jesus. Holy Mary, Mother of God, pray for us sinners, now and at the hour of our death. Amen.

IX. Hail Mary, full of Grace, the Lord is with thee. Blessed art thou among women, and blessed is the fruit of thy womb, Jesus. Holy Mary, Mother of God, pray for us sinners, now and at the hour of our death. Amen.

X. Hail Mary, full of Grace, the Lord is with thee. Blessed art thou among women, and blessed is the fruit of thy womb, Jesus. Holy Mary, Mother of God, pray for us sinners, now and at the hour of our death. Amen.

Glory be to the Father, and to the Son, and to the Holy Spirit. As it was in the beginning, is now, and ever shall be, world without end. Amen.

O my Jesus, forgive us our sins, save us from the fires of hell, lead all souls to heaven, especially those in most need of Thy mercy. Amen.

May the Grace of this Mystery come down into my soul. Amen.

The Second Joyful Mystery;
"The Visitation"

(Spiritual Fruit: Love of Neighbor)

Thereupon Mary set out, proceeding in haste into the hill country to a town of Judah, where she entered Zechariah's house and greeted Elizabeth. (Luke 1:39-40)

Our Father, Who art in heaven, Hallowed be Thy name; Thy kingdom come; Thy will be done on earth as it is in heaven. Give us this day our daily bread; and forgive us our trespasses as we forgive those who trespass against us; and lead us not into temptation, but deliver us from evil. Amen.

I. Hail Mary, full of Grace, the Lord is with thee. Blessed art thou among women, and blessed is the fruit of thy womb, Jesus. Holy Mary, Mother of God, pray for us sinners, now and at the hour of our death. Amen.

II. Hail Mary, full of Grace, the Lord is with thee. Blessed art thou among women, and blessed is the fruit of thy womb, Jesus. Holy Mary, Mother of God, pray for us sinners, now and at the hour of our death. Amen.

III. Hail Mary, full of Grace, the Lord is with thee. Blessed art thou among women, and blessed is the fruit of thy womb, Jesus. Holy Mary, Mother of God, pray for us sinners, now and at the hour of our death. Amen.

IV. Hail Mary, full of Grace, the Lord is with thee. Blessed art thou among women, and blessed is the fruit of thy womb, Jesus. Holy Mary, Mother of God, pray for us sinners, now and at the hour of our death. Amen.

V.   Hail Mary, full of Grace, the Lord is with thee. Blessed art thou among women, and blessed is the fruit of thy womb, Jesus. Holy Mary, Mother of God, pray for us sinners, now and at the hour of our death. Amen.

VI.   Hail Mary, full of Grace, the Lord is with thee. Blessed art thou among women, and blessed is the fruit of thy womb, Jesus. Holy Mary, Mother of God, pray for us sinners, now and at the hour of our death. Amen.

VII.   Hail Mary, full of Grace, the Lord is with thee. Blessed art thou among women, and blessed is the fruit of thy womb, Jesus. Holy Mary, Mother of God, pray for us sinners, now and at the hour of our death. Amen.

VIII.   Hail Mary, full of Grace, the Lord is with thee. Blessed art thou among women, and blessed is the fruit of thy womb, Jesus. Holy Mary, Mother of God, pray for us sinners, now and at the hour of our death. Amen.

IX.   Hail Mary, full of Grace, the Lord is with thee. Blessed art thou among women, and blessed is the fruit of thy womb, Jesus. Holy Mary, Mother of God, pray for us sinners, now and at the hour of our death. Amen.

X.   Hail Mary, full of Grace, the Lord is with thee. Blessed art thou among women, and blessed is the fruit of thy womb, Jesus. Holy Mary, Mother of God, pray for us sinners, now and at the hour of our death. Amen.

Glory be to the Father, and to the Son, and to the Holy Spirit. As it was in the beginning, is now, and ever shall be, world without end. Amen.

O my Jesus, forgive us our sins, save us from the fires of hell, lead all souls to heaven, especially those in most need of Thy mercy. Amen.

May the Grace of this Mystery come down into my soul. Amen.

The Third Joyful Mystery;
"The Nativity of the Lord"

(Spiritual Fruit: Poverty of Spirit)

Now this is how the birth of Jesus Christ came about. When His mother Mary was engaged to Joseph, but before they lived together, she was found with child through the power of the Holy Spirit. (Matthew 1:18)

Our Father, Who art in heaven, Hallowed be Thy name; Thy kingdom come; Thy will be done on earth as it is in heaven. Give us this day our daily bread; and forgive us our trespasses as we forgive those who trespass against us; and lead us not into temptation, but deliver us from evil. Amen.

I. Hail Mary, full of Grace, the Lord is with thee. Blessed art thou among women, and blessed is the fruit of thy womb, Jesus. Holy Mary, Mother of God, pray for us sinners, now and at the hour of our death. Amen.

II. Hail Mary, full of Grace, the Lord is with thee. Blessed art thou among women, and blessed is the fruit of thy womb, Jesus. Holy Mary, Mother of God, pray for us sinners, now and at the hour of our death. Amen.

III. Hail Mary, full of Grace, the Lord is with thee. Blessed art thou among women, and blessed is the fruit of thy womb, Jesus. Holy Mary, Mother of God, pray for us sinners, now and at the hour of our death. Amen.

IV. Hail Mary, full of Grace, the Lord is with thee. Blessed art thou among women, and blessed is the fruit of thy womb, Jesus. Holy Mary, Mother of God, pray for us sinners, now and at the hour of our death. Amen.

V.   Hail Mary, full of Grace, the Lord is with thee. Blessed art thou among women, and blessed is the fruit of thy womb, Jesus. Holy Mary, Mother of God, pray for us sinners, now and at the hour of our death. Amen.

VI.   Hail Mary, full of Grace, the Lord is with thee. Blessed art thou among women, and blessed is the fruit of thy womb, Jesus. Holy Mary, Mother of God, pray for us sinners, now and at the hour of our death. Amen.

VII. Hail Mary, full of Grace, the Lord is with thee. Blessed art thou among women, and blessed is the fruit of thy womb, Jesus. Holy Mary, Mother of God, pray for us sinners, now and at the hour of our death. Amen.

VIII. Hail Mary, full of Grace, the Lord is with thee. Blessed art thou among women, and blessed is the fruit of thy womb, Jesus. Holy Mary, Mother of God, pray for us sinners, now and at the hour of our death. Amen.

IX.   Hail Mary, full of Grace, the Lord is with thee. Blessed art thou among women, and blessed is the fruit of thy womb, Jesus. Holy Mary, Mother of God, pray for us sinners, now and at the hour of our death. Amen.

X.   Hail Mary, full of Grace, the Lord is with thee. Blessed art thou among women, and blessed is the fruit of thy womb, Jesus. Holy Mary, Mother of God, pray for us sinners, now and at the hour of our death. Amen.

Glory be to the Father, and to the Son, and to the Holy Spirit. As it was in the beginning, is now, and ever shall be, world without end. Amen.

O my Jesus, forgive us our sins, save us from the fires of hell, lead all souls to heaven, especially those in most need of Thy mercy. Amen.

May the Grace of this Mystery come down into my soul. Amen.

The Fourth Joyful Mystery;
"The Presentation of the Lord"

(Spiritual Fruit: Purity of Mind & Body)

When the day came to purify them according to the law of Moses, the couple brought Him up to Jerusalem so that He could be presented to the Lord. (Luke 2:22)

Our Father, Who art in heaven, Hallowed be Thy name; Thy kingdom come; Thy will be done on earth as it is in heaven. Give us this day our daily bread; and forgive us our trespasses as we forgive those who trespass against us; and lead us not into temptation, but deliver us from evil. Amen.

I. Hail Mary, full of Grace, the Lord is with thee. Blessed art thou among women, and blessed is the fruit of thy womb, Jesus. Holy Mary, Mother of God, pray for us sinners, now and at the hour of our death. Amen.

II. Hail Mary, full of Grace, the Lord is with thee. Blessed art thou among women, and blessed is the fruit of thy womb, Jesus. Holy Mary, Mother of God, pray for us sinners, now and at the hour of our death. Amen.

III. Hail Mary, full of Grace, the Lord is with thee. Blessed art thou among women, and blessed is the fruit of thy womb, Jesus. Holy Mary, Mother of God, pray for us sinners, now and at the hour of our death. Amen.

IV. Hail Mary, full of Grace, the Lord is with thee. Blessed art thou among women, and blessed is the fruit of thy womb, Jesus. Holy Mary, Mother of God, pray for us sinners, now and at the hour of our death. Amen.

V.   Hail Mary, full of Grace, the Lord is with thee. Blessed art thou among women, and blessed is the fruit of thy womb, Jesus. Holy Mary, Mother of God, pray for us sinners, now and at the hour of our death. Amen.

VI.   Hail Mary, full of Grace, the Lord is with thee. Blessed art thou among women, and blessed is the fruit of thy womb, Jesus. Holy Mary, Mother of God, pray for us sinners, now and at the hour of our death. Amen.

VII. Hail Mary, full of Grace, the Lord is with thee. Blessed art thou among women, and blessed is the fruit of thy womb, Jesus. Holy Mary, Mother of God, pray for us sinners, now and at the hour of our death. Amen.

VIII. Hail Mary, full of Grace, the Lord is with thee. Blessed art thou among women, and blessed is the fruit of thy womb, Jesus. Holy Mary, Mother of God, pray for us sinners, now and at the hour of our death. Amen.

IX.   Hail Mary, full of Grace, the Lord is with thee. Blessed art thou among women, and blessed is the fruit of thy womb, Jesus. Holy Mary, Mother of God, pray for us sinners, now and at the hour of our death. Amen.

X.   Hail Mary, full of Grace, the Lord is with thee. Blessed art thou among women, and blessed is the fruit of thy womb, Jesus. Holy Mary, Mother of God, pray for us sinners, now and at the hour of our death. Amen.

Glory be to the Father, and to the Son, and to the Holy Spirit. As it was in the beginning, is now, and ever shall be, world without end. Amen.

O my Jesus, forgive us our sins, save us from the fires of hell, lead all souls to heaven, especially those in most need of Thy mercy. Amen.

May the Grace of this Mystery come down into my soul. Amen.

The Fifth Joyful Mystery;
"The Finding in the Temple"

(Spiritual Fruit: Obedience)

As they were returning at the end of the feast, the child Jesus remained behind unknown to His parents. (Luke 2:43)

Our Father, Who art in heaven, Hallowed be Thy name; Thy kingdom come; Thy will be done on earth as it is in heaven. Give us this day our daily bread; and forgive us our trespasses as we forgive those who trespass against us; and lead us not into temptation, but deliver us from evil. Amen.

I. Hail Mary, full of Grace, the Lord is with thee. Blessed art thou among women, and blessed is the fruit of thy womb, Jesus. Holy Mary, Mother of God, pray for us sinners, now and at the hour of our death. Amen.

II. Hail Mary, full of Grace, the Lord is with thee. Blessed art thou among women, and blessed is the fruit of thy womb, Jesus. Holy Mary, Mother of God, pray for us sinners, now and at the hour of our death. Amen.

III. Hail Mary, full of Grace, the Lord is with thee. Blessed art thou among women, and blessed is the fruit of thy womb, Jesus. Holy Mary, Mother of God, pray for us sinners, now and at the hour of our death. Amen.

IV. Hail Mary, full of Grace, the Lord is with thee. Blessed art thou among women, and blessed is the fruit of thy womb, Jesus. Holy Mary, Mother of God, pray for us sinners, now and at the hour of our death. Amen.

V.   Hail Mary, full of Grace, the Lord is with thee. Blessed art thou among women, and blessed is the fruit of thy womb, Jesus. Holy Mary, Mother of God, pray for us sinners, now and at the hour of our death. Amen.

VI.   Hail Mary, full of Grace, the Lord is with thee. Blessed art thou among women, and blessed is the fruit of thy womb, Jesus. Holy Mary, Mother of God, pray for us sinners, now and at the hour of our death. Amen.

VII. Hail Mary, full of Grace, the Lord is with thee. Blessed art thou among women, and blessed is the fruit of thy womb, Jesus. Holy Mary, Mother of God, pray for us sinners, now and at the hour of our death. Amen.

VIII. Hail Mary, full of Grace, the Lord is with thee. Blessed art thou among women, and blessed is the fruit of thy womb, Jesus. Holy Mary, Mother of God, pray for us sinners, now and at the hour of our death. Amen.

IX.   Hail Mary, full of Grace, the Lord is with thee. Blessed art thou among women, and blessed is the fruit of thy womb, Jesus. Holy Mary, Mother of God, pray for us sinners, now and at the hour of our death. Amen.

X.   Hail Mary, full of Grace, the Lord is with thee. Blessed art thou among women, and blessed is the fruit of thy womb, Jesus. Holy Mary, Mother of God, pray for us sinners, now and at the hour of our death. Amen.

Glory be to the Father, and to the Son, and to the Holy Spirit. As it was in the beginning, is now, and ever shall be, world without end. Amen.

O my Jesus, forgive us our sins, save us from the fires of hell, lead all souls to heaven, especially those in most need of Thy mercy. Amen.

May the Grace of this Mystery come down into my soul. Amen.

Hail, Holy Queen, Mother of Mercy, our life, our sweetness and our hope. To you do we cry, poor banished children of Eve. To you do we send up our sighs, mourning and weeping in this valley of tears. Turn then most gracious advocate, your eyes of mercy toward us; and after this, our exile, show unto us the blessed fruit of your womb, Jesus. O clement, O loving, O sweet Virgin Mary.

V. Pray for us, O Holy Mother of God,
R. That we may be made worthy of the promises of Christ.

Let us pray. O God, whose only-begotten Son, by His life death, and resurrection, has purchased for us the rewards of eternal life, grant, we beseech Thee, that by meditating upon these Mysteries of the Most Holy Rosary of the Blessed Virgin Mary, we may imitate what they contain and obtain what they promise, through the same Christ our Lord. Amen.

My God, I believe, I adore, I hope, and I love You. I beg pardon of You for those who do not believe, do not adore, do not hope and do not love You.

St. Michael the Archangel, defend us in battle. Be our defense against the wickedness and snares of the Devil. May God rebuke him, we humbly pray, and do thou, O Prince of thy heavenly hosts, by the power of God, thrust into hell Satan and all the other evil spirits, who prowl about the world seeking the ruin of souls. Amen.

Queen of the Rosary, sweet Virgin of Fatima, who hast deigned to appear in the land of Portugal and hast brought peace, both interior and exterior, to that once so troubled country, we beg of thee to watch over our dear homeland and to assure its moral and spiritual revival.

Bring back peace to all nations of the world, so that all, and our own nation in particular, may be happy to call thee their Queen and the Queen of Peace.

Our Lady of the Rosary, pray for our country. Our Lady of Fatima, obtain for all humanity a durable peace. Amen.

In the name of the Father, and of the Son, and of the Holy Spirit. Amen.

The Luminous Mysteries

In the name of the Father, and of the Son, and of the Holy Spirit. Amen.

Queen of the Holy Rosary, you have deigned to come to Fatima to reveal to the three shepherd children the treasures of Grace hidden in the Rosary. Inspire my heart with a sincere love of this devotion, in order that by meditating on the Mysteries of our Redemption which are recalled in it, I may be enriched with its fruits and obtain peace for the world, the conversion of sinners and of Russia, and the favour which I ask of you in this Rosary.

(Here mention your petition)

I ask for this for the greater glory of God, for Thine own honour, and for the good of souls, especially for my own. Amen.

I offer this Rosary for the purpose of knowing the Truth and obtaining contrition and pardon for my sins. Amen.

I believe in God, the Father Almighty, Creator of heaven and earth, and in Jesus Christ, His only Son, our Lord, who was conceived by the Holy Spirit, born of the Virgin Mary, suffered under Pontius Pilate, was crucified, died and was buried; He descended into hell; on the third day He rose again from the dead; He ascended into heaven, and is seated at the right hand of God the Father Almighty; from there He will come

to judge the living and the dead. I believe in the Holy Spirit, the Holy Catholic Church, the communion of saints, the forgiveness of sins, the resurrection of the body and life everlasting. Amen.

Our Father, Who art in heaven, Hallowed be Thy name; Thy kingdom come; Thy will be done on earth as it is in heaven. Give us this day our daily bread; and forgive us our trespasses as we forgive those who trespass against us; and lead us not into temptation, but deliver us from evil. Amen.

I.   Hail Mary, full of Grace, the Lord is with thee. Blessed art thou among women, and blessed is the fruit of thy womb, Jesus. Holy Mary, Mother of God, pray for us sinners, now and at the hour of our death. Amen.

II.   Hail Mary, full of Grace, the Lord is with thee. Blessed art thou among women, and blessed is the fruit of thy womb, Jesus. Holy Mary, Mother of God, pray for us sinners, now and at the hour of our death. Amen.

III. Hail Mary, full of Grace, the Lord is with thee. Blessed art thou among women, and blessed is the fruit of thy womb, Jesus. Holy Mary, Mother of God, pray for us sinners, now and at the hour of our death. Amen.

Glory be to the Father, and to the Son, and to the Holy Spirit. As it was in the beginning, is now, and ever shall be, world without end. Amen.

O my Jesus, forgive us our sins, save us from the fires of hell, lead all souls to heaven, especially those in most need of Thy mercy. Amen.

The First Luminous Mystery;
"The Baptism of Jesus"

(Spiritual Fruit: Openness to the Holy Spirit)

Thus it was that John the Baptizer appeared in the desert, proclaiming a baptism of repentance which led to the forgiveness of sins. (Mark 1:4)

Our Father, Who art in heaven, Hallowed be Thy name; Thy kingdom come; Thy will be done on earth as it is in heaven. Give us this day our daily bread; and forgive us our trespasses as we forgive those who trespass against us; and lead us not into temptation, but deliver us from evil. Amen.

I.   Hail Mary, full of Grace, the Lord is with thee. Blessed art thou among women, and blessed is the fruit of thy womb, Jesus. Holy Mary, Mother of God, pray for us sinners, now and at the hour of our death. Amen.

II.   Hail Mary, full of Grace, the Lord is with thee. Blessed art thou among women, and blessed is the fruit of thy womb, Jesus. Holy Mary, Mother of God, pray for us sinners, now and at the hour of our death. Amen.

III.   Hail Mary, full of Grace, the Lord is with thee. Blessed art thou among women, and blessed is the fruit of thy womb, Jesus. Holy Mary, Mother of God, pray for us sinners, now and at the hour of our death. Amen.

IV.   Hail Mary, full of Grace, the Lord is with thee. Blessed art thou among women, and blessed is the fruit of thy womb, Jesus. Holy Mary, Mother of God, pray for us sinners, now and at the hour of our death. Amen.

V. Hail Mary, full of Grace, the Lord is with thee. Blessed art thou among women, and blessed is the fruit of thy womb, Jesus. Holy Mary, Mother of God, pray for us sinners, now and at the hour of our death. Amen.

VI. Hail Mary, full of Grace, the Lord is with thee. Blessed art thou among women, and blessed is the fruit of thy womb, Jesus. Holy Mary, Mother of God, pray for us sinners, now and at the hour of our death. Amen.

VII. Hail Mary, full of Grace, the Lord is with thee. Blessed art thou among women, and blessed is the fruit of thy womb, Jesus. Holy Mary, Mother of God, pray for us sinners, now and at the hour of our death. Amen.

VIII. Hail Mary, full of Grace, the Lord is with thee. Blessed art thou among women, and blessed is the fruit of thy womb, Jesus. Holy Mary, Mother of God, pray for us sinners, now and at the hour of our death. Amen.

IX. Hail Mary, full of Grace, the Lord is with thee. Blessed art thou among women, and blessed is the fruit of thy womb, Jesus. Holy Mary, Mother of God, pray for us sinners, now and at the hour of our death. Amen.

X. Hail Mary, full of Grace, the Lord is with thee. Blessed art thou among women, and blessed is the fruit of thy womb, Jesus. Holy Mary, Mother of God, pray for us sinners, now and at the hour of our death. Amen.

Glory be to the Father, and to the Son, and to the Holy Spirit. As it was in the beginning, is now, and ever shall be, world without end. Amen.

O my Jesus, forgive us our sins, save us from the fires of hell, lead all souls to heaven, especially those in most need of Thy mercy. Amen.

May the Grace of this Mystery come down into my soul. Amen.

The Second Luminous Mystery; "The Wedding Feast at Cana"

(Spiritual Fruit: Faith in Mary's Intercessory Power with our Lord)

On the third day there was a wedding at Cana in Galilee, and the mother of Jesus was there. Jesus and His disciples had likewise been invited to the celebration. (John 2:1-2)

Our Father, Who art in heaven, Hallowed be Thy name; Thy kingdom come; Thy will be done on earth as it is in heaven. Give us this day our daily bread; and forgive us our trespasses as we forgive those who trespass against us; and lead us not into temptation, but deliver us from evil. Amen.

I. Hail Mary, full of Grace, the Lord is with thee. Blessed art thou among women, and blessed is the fruit of thy womb, Jesus. Holy Mary, Mother of God, pray for us sinners, now and at the hour of our death. Amen.

II. Hail Mary, full of Grace, the Lord is with thee. Blessed art thou among women, and blessed is the fruit of thy womb, Jesus. Holy Mary, Mother of God, pray for us sinners, now and at the hour of our death. Amen.

III. Hail Mary, full of Grace, the Lord is with thee. Blessed art thou among women, and blessed is the fruit of thy womb, Jesus. Holy Mary, Mother of God, pray for us sinners, now and at the hour of our death. Amen.

IV. Hail Mary, full of Grace, the Lord is with thee. Blessed art thou among women, and blessed is the fruit of thy womb, Jesus. Holy Mary, Mother of God, pray for us sinners, now and at the hour of our death. Amen.

V.   Hail Mary, full of Grace, the Lord is with thee. Blessed art thou among women, and blessed is the fruit of thy womb, Jesus. Holy Mary, Mother of God, pray for us sinners, now and at the hour of our death. Amen.

VI.   Hail Mary, full of Grace, the Lord is with thee. Blessed art thou among women, and blessed is the fruit of thy womb, Jesus. Holy Mary, Mother of God, pray for us sinners, now and at the hour of our death. Amen.

VII.   Hail Mary, full of Grace, the Lord is with thee. Blessed art thou among women, and blessed is the fruit of thy womb, Jesus. Holy Mary, Mother of God, pray for us sinners, now and at the hour of our death. Amen.

VIII.   Hail Mary, full of Grace, the Lord is with thee. Blessed art thou among women, and blessed is the fruit of thy womb, Jesus. Holy Mary, Mother of God, pray for us sinners, now and at the hour of our death. Amen.

IX.   Hail Mary, full of Grace, the Lord is with thee. Blessed art thou among women, and blessed is the fruit of thy womb, Jesus. Holy Mary, Mother of God, pray for us sinners, now and at the hour of our death. Amen.

X.   Hail Mary, full of Grace, the Lord is with thee. Blessed art thou among women, and blessed is the fruit of thy womb, Jesus. Holy Mary, Mother of God, pray for us sinners, now and at the hour of our death. Amen.

Glory be to the Father, and to the Son, and to the Holy Spirit. As it was in the beginning, is now, and ever shall be, world without end. Amen.

O my Jesus, forgive us our sins, save us from the fires of hell, lead all souls to heaven, especially those in most need of Thy mercy. Amen.

May the Grace of this Mystery come down into my soul. Amen.

The Third Luminous Mystery;
"The Proclamation of the Kingdom of God"

(Spiritual Fruit: Desire for Holiness; Coming of God's Kingdom on Earth)

After John's arrest, Jesus appeared in Galilee proclaiming the good news of God, "This is the time of fulfillment. The reign of God is at hand! Reform your lives and believe in the gospel." (Mark 1:14-15)

Our Father, Who art in heaven, Hallowed be Thy name; Thy kingdom come; Thy will be done on earth as it is in heaven. Give us this day our daily bread; and forgive us our trespasses as we forgive those who trespass against us; and lead us not into temptation, but deliver us from evil. Amen.

I.   Hail Mary, full of Grace, the Lord is with thee. Blessed art thou among women, and blessed is the fruit of thy womb, Jesus. Holy Mary, Mother of God, pray for us sinners, now and at the hour of our death. Amen.

II.   Hail Mary, full of Grace, the Lord is with thee. Blessed art thou among women, and blessed is the fruit of thy womb, Jesus. Holy Mary, Mother of God, pray for us sinners, now and at the hour of our death. Amen.

III.   Hail Mary, full of Grace, the Lord is with thee. Blessed art thou among women, and blessed is the fruit of thy womb, Jesus. Holy Mary, Mother of God, pray for us sinners, now and at the hour of our death. Amen.

IV.   Hail Mary, full of Grace, the Lord is with thee. Blessed art thou among women, and blessed is the fruit of thy womb, Jesus. Holy Mary, Mother of God, pray for us sinners, now and at the hour of our death. Amen.

V.   Hail Mary, full of Grace, the Lord is with thee. Blessed art thou among women, and blessed is the fruit of thy womb, Jesus. Holy Mary, Mother of God, pray for us sinners, now and at the hour of our death. Amen.

VI.   Hail Mary, full of Grace, the Lord is with thee. Blessed art thou among women, and blessed is the fruit of thy womb, Jesus. Holy Mary, Mother of God, pray for us sinners, now and at the hour of our death. Amen.

VII.   Hail Mary, full of Grace, the Lord is with thee. Blessed art thou among women, and blessed is the fruit of thy womb, Jesus. Holy Mary, Mother of God, pray for us sinners, now and at the hour of our death. Amen.

VIII.   Hail Mary, full of Grace, the Lord is with thee. Blessed art thou among women, and blessed is the fruit of thy womb, Jesus. Holy Mary, Mother of God, pray for us sinners, now and at the hour of our death. Amen.

IX.   Hail Mary, full of Grace, the Lord is with thee. Blessed art thou among women, and blessed is the fruit of thy womb, Jesus. Holy Mary, Mother of God, pray for us sinners, now and at the hour of our death. Amen.

X.   Hail Mary, full of Grace, the Lord is with thee. Blessed art thou among women, and blessed is the fruit of thy womb, Jesus. Holy Mary, Mother of God, pray for us sinners, now and at the hour of our death. Amen.

Glory be to the Father, and to the Son, and to the Holy Spirit. As it was in the beginning, is now, and ever shall be, world without end. Amen.

O my Jesus, forgive us our sins, save us from the fires of hell, lead all souls to heaven, especially those in most need of Thy mercy. Amen.

May the Grace of this Mystery come down into my soul. Amen.

The Fourth Luminous Mystery; "The Transfiguration"

(Spiritual Fruit; Acknowledgement of Christ's Divinity)

Six days later, Jesus took Peter, James, and John off by themselves with Him and led them up a high mountain. He was transfigured before their eyes. (Mark 9:2)

Our Father, Who art in heaven, Hallowed be Thy name; Thy kingdom come; Thy will be done on earth as it is in heaven. Give us this day our daily bread; and forgive us our trespasses as we forgive those who trespass against us; and lead us not into temptation, but deliver us from evil. Amen.

I. Hail Mary, full of Grace, the Lord is with thee. Blessed art thou among women, and blessed is the fruit of thy womb, Jesus. Holy Mary, Mother of God, pray for us sinners, now and at the hour of our death. Amen.

II. Hail Mary, full of Grace, the Lord is with thee. Blessed art thou among women, and blessed is the fruit of thy womb, Jesus. Holy Mary, Mother of God, pray for us sinners, now and at the hour of our death. Amen.

III. Hail Mary, full of Grace, the Lord is with thee. Blessed art thou among women, and blessed is the fruit of thy womb, Jesus. Holy Mary, Mother of God, pray for us sinners, now and at the hour of our death. Amen.

IV. Hail Mary, full of Grace, the Lord is with thee. Blessed art thou among women, and blessed is the fruit of thy womb, Jesus. Holy Mary, Mother of God, pray for us sinners, now and at the hour of our death. Amen.

V. Hail Mary, full of Grace, the Lord is with thee. Blessed art thou among women, and blessed is the fruit of thy womb, Jesus. Holy Mary, Mother of God, pray for us sinners, now and at the hour of our death. Amen.

VI. Hail Mary, full of Grace, the Lord is with thee. Blessed art thou among women, and blessed is the fruit of thy womb, Jesus. Holy Mary, Mother of God, pray for us sinners, now and at the hour of our death. Amen.

VII. Hail Mary, full of Grace, the Lord is with thee. Blessed art thou among women, and blessed is the fruit of thy womb, Jesus. Holy Mary, Mother of God, pray for us sinners, now and at the hour of our death. Amen.

VIII. Hail Mary, full of Grace, the Lord is with thee. Blessed art thou among women, and blessed is the fruit of thy womb, Jesus. Holy Mary, Mother of God, pray for us sinners, now and at the hour of our death. Amen.

IX. Hail Mary, full of Grace, the Lord is with thee. Blessed art thou among women, and blessed is the fruit of thy womb, Jesus. Holy Mary, Mother of God, pray for us sinners, now and at the hour of our death. Amen.

X. Hail Mary, full of Grace, the Lord is with thee. Blessed art thou among women, and blessed is the fruit of thy womb, Jesus. Holy Mary, Mother of God, pray for us sinners, now and at the hour of our death. Amen.

Glory be to the Father, and to the Son, and to the Holy Spirit. As it was in the beginning, is now, and ever shall be, world without end. Amen.

O my Jesus, forgive us our sins, save us from the fires of hell, lead all souls to heaven, especially those in most need of Thy mercy. Amen.

May the Grace of this Mystery come down into my soul. Amen.

The Fifth Luminous Mystery;
"The Institution of the Eucharist"

(Spiritual Fruit: Reverence and Love for our Lord in the Eucharist)

When the hour arrived, He took His place at the table, and the apostles with Him. He said to them, "I have greatly desired to eat this Passover with you before I suffer." (Luke 22:14-15)

Our Father, Who art in heaven, Hallowed be Thy name; Thy kingdom come; Thy will be done on earth as it is in heaven. Give us this day our daily bread; and forgive us our trespasses as we forgive those who trespass against us; and lead us not into temptation, but deliver us from evil. Amen.

I. Hail Mary, full of Grace, the Lord is with thee. Blessed art thou among women, and blessed is the fruit of thy womb, Jesus. Holy Mary, Mother of God, pray for us sinners, now and at the hour of our death. Amen.

II. Hail Mary, full of Grace, the Lord is with thee. Blessed art thou among women, and blessed is the fruit of thy womb, Jesus. Holy Mary, Mother of God, pray for us sinners, now and at the hour of our death. Amen.

III. Hail Mary, full of Grace, the Lord is with thee. Blessed art thou among women, and blessed is the fruit of thy womb, Jesus. Holy Mary, Mother of God, pray for us sinners, now and at the hour of our death. Amen.

IV. Hail Mary, full of Grace, the Lord is with thee. Blessed art thou among women, and blessed is the fruit of thy womb, Jesus. Holy Mary, Mother of God, pray for us sinners, now and at the hour of our death. Amen.

V.   Hail Mary, full of Grace, the Lord is with thee. Blessed art thou among women, and blessed is the fruit of thy womb, Jesus. Holy Mary, Mother of God, pray for us sinners, now and at the hour of our death. Amen.

VI.   Hail Mary, full of Grace, the Lord is with thee. Blessed art thou among women, and blessed is the fruit of thy womb, Jesus. Holy Mary, Mother of God, pray for us sinners, now and at the hour of our death. Amen.

VII.   Hail Mary, full of Grace, the Lord is with thee. Blessed art thou among women, and blessed is the fruit of thy womb, Jesus. Holy Mary, Mother of God, pray for us sinners, now and at the hour of our death. Amen.

VIII.   Hail Mary, full of Grace, the Lord is with thee. Blessed art thou among women, and blessed is the fruit of thy womb, Jesus. Holy Mary, Mother of God, pray for us sinners, now and at the hour of our death. Amen.

IX.   Hail Mary, full of Grace, the Lord is with thee. Blessed art thou among women, and blessed is the fruit of thy womb, Jesus. Holy Mary, Mother of God, pray for us sinners, now and at the hour of our death. Amen.

X.   Hail Mary, full of Grace, the Lord is with thee. Blessed art thou among women, and blessed is the fruit of thy womb, Jesus. Holy Mary, Mother of God, pray for us sinners, now and at the hour of our death. Amen.

Glory be to the Father, and to the Son, and to the Holy Spirit. As it was in the beginning, is now, and ever shall be, world without end. Amen.

O my Jesus, forgive us our sins, save us from the fires of hell, lead all souls to heaven, especially those in most need of Thy mercy. Amen.

May the Grace of this Mystery come down into my soul. Amen.

Hail, Holy Queen, Mother of Mercy, our life, our sweetness and our hope. To you do we cry, poor banished children of Eve. To you do we send up our sighs, mourning and weeping in this valley of tears. Turn then most gracious advocate, your eyes of mercy toward us; and after this, our exile, show unto us the blessed fruit of your womb, Jesus. O clement, O loving, O sweet Virgin Mary.

V. Pray for us, O Holy Mother of God,
R. That we may be made worthy of the promises of Christ.

Let us pray. O God, whose only-begotten Son, by His life death, and resurrection, has purchased for us the rewards of eternal life, grant, we beseech Thee, that by meditating upon these Mysteries of the Most Holy Rosary of the Blessed Virgin Mary, we may imitate what they contain and obtain what they promise, through the same Christ our Lord. Amen.

My God, I believe, I adore, I hope, and I love You. I beg pardon of You for those who do not believe, do not adore, do not hope and do not love You.

St. Michael the Archangel, defend us in battle. Be our defense against the wickedness and snares of the Devil. May God rebuke him, we humbly pray, and do thou, O Prince of thy heavenly hosts, by the power of God, thrust into hell Satan and all the other evil spirits, who prowl about the world seeking the ruin of souls. Amen.

Queen of the Rosary, sweet Virgin of Fatima, who hast deigned to appear in the land of Portugal and hast brought peace, both interior and exterior, to that once so troubled country, we beg of thee to watch over our dear homeland and to assure its moral and spiritual revival.

Bring back peace to all nations of the world, so that all, and our own nation in particular, may be happy to call thee their Queen and the Queen of Peace.

Our Lady of the Rosary, pray for our country. Our Lady of Fatima, obtain for all humanity a durable peace. Amen.

In the name of the Father, and of the Son, and of the Holy Spirit. Amen.

The Sorrowful Mysteries

In the name of the Father, and of the Son, and of the Holy Spirit. Amen.

Queen of the Holy Rosary, you have deigned to come to Fatima to reveal to the three shepherd children the treasures of Grace hidden in the Rosary. Inspire my heart with a sincere love of this devotion, in order that by meditating on the Mysteries of our Redemption which are recalled in it, I may be enriched with its fruits and obtain peace for the world, the conversion of sinners and of Russia, and the favour which I ask of you in this Rosary.

(Here mention your petition)

I ask for this for the greater glory of God, for Thine own honour, and for the good of souls, especially for my own. Amen.

I offer this Rosary for the purpose of knowing the Truth and obtaining contrition and pardon for my sins. Amen.

I believe in God, the Father Almighty, Creator of heaven and earth, and in Jesus Christ, His only Son, our Lord, who was conceived by the Holy Spirit, born of the Virgin Mary, suffered under Pontius Pilate, was crucified, died and was buried; He descended into hell; on the third day He rose again from the dead; He ascended into heaven, and is seated at the right hand of God the Father Almighty; from there He will come

to judge the living and the dead. I believe in the Holy Spirit, the Holy Catholic Church, the communion of saints, the forgiveness of sins, the resurrection of the body and life everlasting. Amen.

Our Father, Who art in heaven, Hallowed be Thy name; Thy kingdom come; Thy will be done on earth as it is in heaven. Give us this day our daily bread; and forgive us our trespasses as we forgive those who trespass against us; and lead us not into temptation, but deliver us from evil. Amen.

I.   Hail Mary, full of Grace, the Lord is with thee. Blessed art thou among women, and blessed is the fruit of thy womb, Jesus. Holy Mary, Mother of God, pray for us sinners, now and at the hour of our death. Amen.

II.   Hail Mary, full of Grace, the Lord is with thee. Blessed art thou among women, and blessed is the fruit of thy womb, Jesus. Holy Mary, Mother of God, pray for us sinners, now and at the hour of our death. Amen.

III.   Hail Mary, full of Grace, the Lord is with thee. Blessed art thou among women, and blessed is the fruit of thy womb, Jesus. Holy Mary, Mother of God, pray for us sinners, now and at the hour of our death. Amen.

Glory be to the Father, and to the Son, and to the Holy Spirit. As it was in the beginning, is now, and ever shall be, world without end. Amen.

O my Jesus, forgive us our sins, save us from the fires of hell, lead all souls to heaven, especially those in most need of Thy mercy. Amen.

The First Sorrowful Mystery;
"The Agony in the Garden"

(Spiritual Fruit; Sorrow for Sin)

While He was still speaking Judas came; and with him a crowd with swords and clubs; And he kissed Him. And they laid hands on Him and seized Him. (Mark 14:45,46)

Our Father, Who art in heaven, Hallowed be Thy name; Thy kingdom come; Thy will be done on earth as it is in heaven. Give us this day our daily bread; and forgive us our trespasses as we forgive those who trespass against us; and lead us not into temptation, but deliver us from evil. Amen.

I.   Hail Mary, full of Grace, the Lord is with thee. Blessed art thou among women, and blessed is the fruit of thy womb, Jesus. Holy Mary, Mother of God, pray for us sinners, now and at the hour of our death. Amen.

II.   Hail Mary, full of Grace, the Lord is with thee. Blessed art thou among women, and blessed is the fruit of thy womb, Jesus. Holy Mary, Mother of God, pray for us sinners, now and at the hour of our death. Amen.

III. Hail Mary, full of Grace, the Lord is with thee. Blessed art thou among women, and blessed is the fruit of thy womb, Jesus. Holy Mary, Mother of God, pray for us sinners, now and at the hour of our death. Amen.

IV.   Hail Mary, full of Grace, the Lord is with thee. Blessed art thou among women, and blessed is the fruit of thy womb, Jesus. Holy Mary, Mother of God, pray for us sinners, now and at the hour of our death. Amen.

V.   Hail Mary, full of Grace, the Lord is with thee. Blessed art thou among women, and blessed is the fruit of thy womb, Jesus. Holy Mary, Mother of God, pray for us sinners, now and at the hour of our death. Amen.

VI.   Hail Mary, full of Grace, the Lord is with thee. Blessed art thou among women, and blessed is the fruit of thy womb, Jesus. Holy Mary, Mother of God, pray for us sinners, now and at the hour of our death. Amen.

VII.   Hail Mary, full of Grace, the Lord is with thee. Blessed art thou among women, and blessed is the fruit of thy womb, Jesus. Holy Mary, Mother of God, pray for us sinners, now and at the hour of our death. Amen.

VIII.   Hail Mary, full of Grace, the Lord is with thee. Blessed art thou among women, and blessed is the fruit of thy womb, Jesus. Holy Mary, Mother of God, pray for us sinners, now and at the hour of our death. Amen.

IX.   Hail Mary, full of Grace, the Lord is with thee. Blessed art thou among women, and blessed is the fruit of thy womb, Jesus. Holy Mary, Mother of God, pray for us sinners, now and at the hour of our death. Amen.

X.   Hail Mary, full of Grace, the Lord is with thee. Blessed art thou among women, and blessed is the fruit of thy womb, Jesus. Holy Mary, Mother of God, pray for us sinners, now and at the hour of our death. Amen.

Glory be to the Father, and to the Son, and to the Holy Spirit. As it was in the beginning, is now, and ever shall be, world without end. Amen.

O my Jesus, forgive us our sins, save us from the fires of hell, lead all souls to heaven, especially those in most need of Thy mercy. Amen.

May the Grace of this Mystery come down into my soul. Amen.

The Second Sorrowful Mystery; "The Scourging"

(Spiritual Fruit; Purity)

Then Pilate took Jesus and scourged Him. (John 19:1)

Our Father, Who art in heaven, Hallowed be Thy name; Thy kingdom come; Thy will be done on earth as it is in heaven. Give us this day our daily bread; and forgive us our trespasses as we forgive those who trespass against us; and lead us not into temptation, but deliver us from evil. Amen.

    I.   Hail Mary, full of Grace, the Lord is with thee. Blessed art thou among women, and blessed is the fruit of thy womb, Jesus. Holy Mary, Mother of God, pray for us sinners, now and at the hour of our death. Amen.

    II.   Hail Mary, full of Grace, the Lord is with thee. Blessed art thou among women, and blessed is the fruit of thy womb, Jesus. Holy Mary, Mother of God, pray for us sinners, now and at the hour of our death. Amen.

    III.   Hail Mary, full of Grace, the Lord is with thee. Blessed art thou among women, and blessed is the fruit of thy womb, Jesus. Holy Mary, Mother of God, pray for us sinners, now and at the hour of our death. Amen.

    IV.   Hail Mary, full of Grace, the Lord is with thee. Blessed art thou among women, and blessed is the fruit of thy womb, Jesus. Holy Mary, Mother of God, pray for us sinners, now and at the hour of our death. Amen.

V.　　Hail Mary, full of Grace, the Lord is with thee. Blessed art thou among women, and blessed is the fruit of thy womb, Jesus. Holy Mary, Mother of God, pray for us sinners, now and at the hour of our death. Amen.

VI.　　Hail Mary, full of Grace, the Lord is with thee. Blessed art thou among women, and blessed is the fruit of thy womb, Jesus. Holy Mary, Mother of God, pray for us sinners, now and at the hour of our death. Amen.

VII.　　Hail Mary, full of Grace, the Lord is with thee. Blessed art thou among women, and blessed is the fruit of thy womb, Jesus. Holy Mary, Mother of God, pray for us sinners, now and at the hour of our death. Amen.

VIII.　　Hail Mary, full of Grace, the Lord is with thee. Blessed art thou among women, and blessed is the fruit of thy womb, Jesus. Holy Mary, Mother of God, pray for us sinners, now and at the hour of our death. Amen.

IX.　　Hail Mary, full of Grace, the Lord is with thee. Blessed art thou among women, and blessed is the fruit of thy womb, Jesus. Holy Mary, Mother of God, pray for us sinners, now and at the hour of our death. Amen.

X.　　Hail Mary, full of Grace, the Lord is with thee. Blessed art thou among women, and blessed is the fruit of thy womb, Jesus. Holy Mary, Mother of God, pray for us sinners, now and at the hour of our death. Amen.

Glory be to the Father, and to the Son, and to the Holy Spirit. As it was in the beginning, is now, and ever shall be, world without end. Amen.

O my Jesus, forgive us our sins, save us from the fires of hell, lead all souls to heaven, especially those in most need of Thy mercy. Amen.

May the Grace of this Mystery come down into my soul. Amen.

The Third Sorrowful Mystery;
"The Crowning with Thorns"

(Spiritual Fruit; Moral Courage)

Continually striking Jesus on the head with a reed and spitting on Him, they genuflected before Him and pretended to pay Him homage. (Mark 15:19)

Our Father, Who art in heaven, Hallowed be Thy name; Thy kingdom come; Thy will be done on earth as it is in heaven. Give us this day our daily bread; and forgive us our trespasses as we forgive those who trespass against us; and lead us not into temptation, but deliver us from evil. Amen.

I.   Hail Mary, full of Grace, the Lord is with thee. Blessed art thou among women, and blessed is the fruit of thy womb, Jesus. Holy Mary, Mother of God, pray for us sinners, now and at the hour of our death. Amen.

II.   Hail Mary, full of Grace, the Lord is with thee. Blessed art thou among women, and blessed is the fruit of thy womb, Jesus. Holy Mary, Mother of God, pray for us sinners, now and at the hour of our death. Amen.

III.   Hail Mary, full of Grace, the Lord is with thee. Blessed art thou among women, and blessed is the fruit of thy womb, Jesus. Holy Mary, Mother of God, pray for us sinners, now and at the hour of our death. Amen.

IV.   Hail Mary, full of Grace, the Lord is with thee. Blessed art thou among women, and blessed is the fruit of thy womb, Jesus. Holy Mary, Mother of God, pray for us sinners, now and at the hour of our death. Amen.

V.   Hail Mary, full of Grace, the Lord is with thee. Blessed art thou among women, and blessed is the fruit of thy womb, Jesus. Holy Mary, Mother of God, pray for us sinners, now and at the hour of our death. Amen.

VI.   Hail Mary, full of Grace, the Lord is with thee. Blessed art thou among women, and blessed is the fruit of thy womb, Jesus. Holy Mary, Mother of God, pray for us sinners, now and at the hour of our death. Amen.

VII.   Hail Mary, full of Grace, the Lord is with thee. Blessed art thou among women, and blessed is the fruit of thy womb, Jesus. Holy Mary, Mother of God, pray for us sinners, now and at the hour of our death. Amen.

VIII.   Hail Mary, full of Grace, the Lord is with thee. Blessed art thou among women, and blessed is the fruit of thy womb, Jesus. Holy Mary, Mother of God, pray for us sinners, now and at the hour of our death. Amen.

IX.   Hail Mary, full of Grace, the Lord is with thee. Blessed art thou among women, and blessed is the fruit of thy womb, Jesus. Holy Mary, Mother of God, pray for us sinners, now and at the hour of our death. Amen.

X.   Hail Mary, full of Grace, the Lord is with thee. Blessed art thou among women, and blessed is the fruit of thy womb, Jesus. Holy Mary, Mother of God, pray for us sinners, now and at the hour of our death. Amen.

Glory be to the Father, and to the Son, and to the Holy Spirit. As it was in the beginning, is now, and ever shall be, world without end. Amen.

O my Jesus, forgive us our sins, save us from the fires of hell, lead all souls to heaven, especially those in most need of Thy mercy. Amen.

May the Grace of this Mystery come down into my soul. Amen.

The Fourth Sorrowful Mystery; "The Carrying of the Cross"

(Spiritual Fruit; Patience)

Carrying the cross by Himself, went out to what is called the Place of the Skull (in Hebrew, Golgotha). (John 19:17)

Our Father, Who art in heaven, Hallowed be Thy name; Thy kingdom come; Thy will be done on earth as it is in heaven. Give us this day our daily bread; and forgive us our trespasses as we forgive those who trespass against us; and lead us not into temptation, but deliver us from evil. Amen.

I. Hail Mary, full of Grace, the Lord is with thee. Blessed art thou among women, and blessed is the fruit of thy womb, Jesus. Holy Mary, Mother of God, pray for us sinners, now and at the hour of our death. Amen.

II. Hail Mary, full of Grace, the Lord is with thee. Blessed art thou among women, and blessed is the fruit of thy womb, Jesus. Holy Mary, Mother of God, pray for us sinners, now and at the hour of our death. Amen.

III. Hail Mary, full of Grace, the Lord is with thee. Blessed art thou among women, and blessed is the fruit of thy womb, Jesus. Holy Mary, Mother of God, pray for us sinners, now and at the hour of our death. Amen.

IV. Hail Mary, full of Grace, the Lord is with thee. Blessed art thou among women, and blessed is the fruit of thy womb, Jesus. Holy Mary, Mother of God, pray for us sinners, now and at the hour of our death. Amen.

V.   Hail Mary, full of Grace, the Lord is with thee. Blessed art thou among women, and blessed is the fruit of thy womb, Jesus. Holy Mary, Mother of God, pray for us sinners, now and at the hour of our death. Amen.

VI.   Hail Mary, full of Grace, the Lord is with thee. Blessed art thou among women, and blessed is the fruit of thy womb, Jesus. Holy Mary, Mother of God, pray for us sinners, now and at the hour of our death. Amen.

VII.   Hail Mary, full of Grace, the Lord is with thee. Blessed art thou among women, and blessed is the fruit of thy womb, Jesus. Holy Mary, Mother of God, pray for us sinners, now and at the hour of our death. Amen.

VIII.   Hail Mary, full of Grace, the Lord is with thee. Blessed art thou among women, and blessed is the fruit of thy womb, Jesus. Holy Mary, Mother of God, pray for us sinners, now and at the hour of our death. Amen.

IX.   Hail Mary, full of Grace, the Lord is with thee. Blessed art thou among women, and blessed is the fruit of thy womb, Jesus. Holy Mary, Mother of God, pray for us sinners, now and at the hour of our death. Amen.

X.   Hail Mary, full of Grace, the Lord is with thee. Blessed art thou among women, and blessed is the fruit of thy womb, Jesus. Holy Mary, Mother of God, pray for us sinners, now and at the hour of our death. Amen.

Glory be to the Father, and to the Son, and to the Holy Spirit. As it was in the beginning, is now, and ever shall be, world without end. Amen.

O my Jesus, forgive us our sins, save us from the fires of hell, lead all souls to heaven, especially those in most need of Thy mercy. Amen.

May the Grace of this Mystery come down into my soul. Amen.

The Fifth Sorrowful Mystery; "The Crucifixion"

(Spiritual Fruit; Perseverance)

Near the cross of Jesus there stood His mother, His mother's sister, Mary the wife of Clopas, and Mary Magdalene. (John 19:25)

Our Father, Who art in heaven, Hallowed be Thy name; Thy kingdom come; Thy will be done on earth as it is in heaven. Give us this day our daily bread; and forgive us our trespasses as we forgive those who trespass against us; and lead us not into temptation, but deliver us from evil. Amen.

I. Hail Mary, full of Grace, the Lord is with thee. Blessed art thou among women, and blessed is the fruit of thy womb, Jesus. Holy Mary, Mother of God, pray for us sinners, now and at the hour of our death. Amen.

II. Hail Mary, full of Grace, the Lord is with thee. Blessed art thou among women, and blessed is the fruit of thy womb, Jesus. Holy Mary, Mother of God, pray for us sinners, now and at the hour of our death. Amen.

III. Hail Mary, full of Grace, the Lord is with thee. Blessed art thou among women, and blessed is the fruit of thy womb, Jesus. Holy Mary, Mother of God, pray for us sinners, now and at the hour of our death. Amen.

IV. Hail Mary, full of Grace, the Lord is with thee. Blessed art thou among women, and blessed is the fruit of thy womb, Jesus. Holy Mary, Mother of God, pray for us sinners, now and at the hour of our death. Amen.

V. Hail Mary, full of Grace, the Lord is with thee. Blessed art thou among women, and blessed is the fruit of thy womb, Jesus. Holy Mary, Mother of God, pray for us sinners, now and at the hour of our death. Amen.

VI. Hail Mary, full of Grace, the Lord is with thee. Blessed art thou among women, and blessed is the fruit of thy womb, Jesus. Holy Mary, Mother of God, pray for us sinners, now and at the hour of our death. Amen.

VII. Hail Mary, full of Grace, the Lord is with thee. Blessed art thou among women, and blessed is the fruit of thy womb, Jesus. Holy Mary, Mother of God, pray for us sinners, now and at the hour of our death. Amen.

VIII. Hail Mary, full of Grace, the Lord is with thee. Blessed art thou among women, and blessed is the fruit of thy womb, Jesus. Holy Mary, Mother of God, pray for us sinners, now and at the hour of our death. Amen.

IX. Hail Mary, full of Grace, the Lord is with thee. Blessed art thou among women, and blessed is the fruit of thy womb, Jesus. Holy Mary, Mother of God, pray for us sinners, now and at the hour of our death. Amen.

X. Hail Mary, full of Grace, the Lord is with thee. Blessed art thou among women, and blessed is the fruit of thy womb, Jesus. Holy Mary, Mother of God, pray for us sinners, now and at the hour of our death. Amen.

Glory be to the Father, and to the Son, and to the Holy Spirit. As it was in the beginning, is now, and ever shall be, world without end. Amen.

O my Jesus, forgive us our sins, save us from the fires of hell, lead all souls to heaven, especially those in most need of Thy mercy. Amen.

May the Grace of this Mystery come down into my soul. Amen.

Hail, Holy Queen, Mother of Mercy, our life, our sweetness and our hope. To you do we cry, poor banished children of Eve. To you do we send up our sighs, mourning and weeping in this valley of tears. Turn then most gracious advocate, your eyes of mercy toward us; and after this, our exile, show unto us the blessed fruit of your womb, Jesus. O clement, O loving, O sweet Virgin Mary.

V. Pray for us, O Holy Mother of God,
R. That we may be made worthy of the promises of Christ.

Let us pray. O God, whose only-begotten Son, by His life death, and resurrection, has purchased for us the rewards of eternal life, grant, we beseech Thee, that by meditating upon these Mysteries of the Most Holy Rosary of the Blessed Virgin Mary, we may imitate what they contain and obtain what they promise, through the same Christ our Lord. Amen.

My God, I believe, I adore, I hope, and I love You. I beg pardon of You for those who do not believe, do not adore, do not hope and do not love You.

St. Michael the Archangel, defend us in battle. Be our defense against the wickedness and snares of the Devil. May God rebuke him, we humbly pray, and do thou, O Prince of thy heavenly hosts, by the power of God, thrust into hell Satan and all the other evil spirits, who prowl about the world seeking the ruin of souls. Amen.

Queen of the Rosary, sweet Virgin of Fatima, who hast deigned to appear in the land of Portugal and hast brought peace, both interior and exterior, to that once so troubled country, we beg of thee to watch over our dear homeland and to assure its moral and spiritual revival.

Bring back peace to all nations of the world, so that all, and our own nation in particular, may be happy to call thee their Queen and the Queen of Peace.

Our Lady of the Rosary, pray for our country. Our Lady of Fatima, obtain for all humanity a durable peace. Amen.

In the name of the Father, and of the Son, and of the Holy Spirit. Amen.

The Glorious Mysteries

In the name of the Father, and of the Son, and of the Holy Spirit. Amen.

Queen of the Holy Rosary, you have deigned to come to Fatima to reveal to the three shepherd children the treasures of Grace hidden in the Rosary. Inspire my heart with a sincere love of this devotion, in order that by meditating on the Mysteries of our Redemption which are recalled in it, I may be enriched with its fruits and obtain peace for the world, the conversion of sinners and of Russia, and the favour which I ask of you in this Rosary.

(Here mention your petition)

I ask for this for the greater glory of God, for Thine own honour, and for the good of souls, especially for my own. Amen.

I offer this Rosary for the purpose of knowing the Truth and obtaining contrition and pardon for my sins. Amen.

I believe in God, the Father Almighty, Creator of heaven and earth, and in Jesus Christ, His only Son, our Lord, who was conceived by the Holy Spirit, born of the Virgin Mary, suffered under Pontius Pilate, was crucified, died and was buried; He descended into hell; on the third day He rose again from the dead; He ascended into heaven, and is seated at the right hand of God the Father Almighty; from there He will come

to judge the living and the dead. I believe in the Holy Spirit, the Holy Catholic Church, the communion of saints, the forgiveness of sins, the resurrection of the body and life everlasting. Amen.

Our Father, Who art in heaven, Hallowed be Thy name; Thy kingdom come; Thy will be done on earth as it is in heaven. Give us this day our daily bread; and forgive us our trespasses as we forgive those who trespass against us; and lead us not into temptation, but deliver us from evil. Amen.

I. Hail Mary, full of Grace, the Lord is with thee. Blessed art thou among women, and blessed is the fruit of thy womb, Jesus. Holy Mary, Mother of God, pray for us sinners, now and at the hour of our death. Amen.

II. Hail Mary, full of Grace, the Lord is with thee. Blessed art thou among women, and blessed is the fruit of thy womb, Jesus. Holy Mary, Mother of God, pray for us sinners, now and at the hour of our death. Amen.

III. Hail Mary, full of Grace, the Lord is with thee. Blessed art thou among women, and blessed is the fruit of thy womb, Jesus. Holy Mary, Mother of God, pray for us sinners, now and at the hour of our death. Amen.

Glory be to the Father, and to the Son, and to the Holy Spirit. As it was in the beginning, is now, and ever shall be, world without end. Amen.

O my Jesus, forgive us our sins, save us from the fires of hell, lead all souls to heaven, especially those in most need of Thy mercy. Amen.

The First Glorious Mystery;
"The Resurrection"

(Spiritual Fruit; Faith)

They found the stone rolled back from the tomb; but when they entered the tomb, they did not find the body of the Lord Jesus. (Luke 24:2-3)

Our Father, Who art in heaven, Hallowed be Thy name; Thy kingdom come; Thy will be done on earth as it is in heaven. Give us this day our daily bread; and forgive us our trespasses as we forgive those who trespass against us; and lead us not into temptation, but deliver us from evil. Amen.

I. Hail Mary, full of Grace, the Lord is with thee. Blessed art thou among women, and blessed is the fruit of thy womb, Jesus. Holy Mary, Mother of God, pray for us sinners, now and at the hour of our death. Amen.

II. Hail Mary, full of Grace, the Lord is with thee. Blessed art thou among women, and blessed is the fruit of thy womb, Jesus. Holy Mary, Mother of God, pray for us sinners, now and at the hour of our death. Amen.

III. Hail Mary, full of Grace, the Lord is with thee. Blessed art thou among women, and blessed is the fruit of thy womb, Jesus. Holy Mary, Mother of God, pray for us sinners, now and at the hour of our death. Amen.

IV. Hail Mary, full of Grace, the Lord is with thee. Blessed art thou among women, and blessed is the fruit of thy womb, Jesus. Holy Mary, Mother of God, pray for us sinners, now and at the hour of our death. Amen.

V.   Hail Mary, full of Grace, the Lord is with thee. Blessed art thou among women, and blessed is the fruit of thy womb, Jesus. Holy Mary, Mother of God, pray for us sinners, now and at the hour of our death. Amen.

VI.   Hail Mary, full of Grace, the Lord is with thee. Blessed art thou among women, and blessed is the fruit of thy womb, Jesus. Holy Mary, Mother of God, pray for us sinners, now and at the hour of our death. Amen.

VII.   Hail Mary, full of Grace, the Lord is with thee. Blessed art thou among women, and blessed is the fruit of thy womb, Jesus. Holy Mary, Mother of God, pray for us sinners, now and at the hour of our death. Amen.

VIII.   Hail Mary, full of Grace, the Lord is with thee. Blessed art thou among women, and blessed is the fruit of thy womb, Jesus. Holy Mary, Mother of God, pray for us sinners, now and at the hour of our death. Amen.

IX.   Hail Mary, full of Grace, the Lord is with thee. Blessed art thou among women, and blessed is the fruit of thy womb, Jesus. Holy Mary, Mother of God, pray for us sinners, now and at the hour of our death. Amen.

X.   Hail Mary, full of Grace, the Lord is with thee. Blessed art thou among women, and blessed is the fruit of thy womb, Jesus. Holy Mary, Mother of God, pray for us sinners, now and at the hour of our death. Amen.

Glory be to the Father, and to the Son, and to the Holy Spirit. As it was in the beginning, is now, and ever shall be, world without end. Amen.

O my Jesus, forgive us our sins, save us from the fires of hell, lead all souls to heaven, especially those in most need of Thy mercy. Amen.

May the Grace of this Mystery come down into my soul. Amen.

The Second Glorious Mystery;
"The Ascension of the Lord"

(Spiritual Fruit; Hope)

And lifting His hands He blessed them. While He blessed them, He parted from them and was taken up into heaven. (Luke 24:50,51)

Our Father, Who art in heaven, Hallowed be Thy name; Thy kingdom come; Thy will be done on earth as it is in heaven. Give us this day our daily bread; and forgive us our trespasses as we forgive those who trespass against us; and lead us not into temptation, but deliver us from evil. Amen.

I.   Hail Mary, full of Grace, the Lord is with thee. Blessed art thou among women, and blessed is the fruit of thy womb, Jesus. Holy Mary, Mother of God, pray for us sinners, now and at the hour of our death. Amen.

II.   Hail Mary, full of Grace, the Lord is with thee. Blessed art thou among women, and blessed is the fruit of thy womb, Jesus. Holy Mary, Mother of God, pray for us sinners, now and at the hour of our death. Amen.

III. Hail Mary, full of Grace, the Lord is with thee. Blessed art thou among women, and blessed is the fruit of thy womb, Jesus. Holy Mary, Mother of God, pray for us sinners, now and at the hour of our death. Amen.

IV.   Hail Mary, full of Grace, the Lord is with thee. Blessed art thou among women, and blessed is the fruit of thy womb, Jesus. Holy Mary, Mother of God, pray for us sinners, now and at the hour of our death. Amen.

V.   Hail Mary, full of Grace, the Lord is with thee. Blessed art thou among women, and blessed is the fruit of thy womb, Jesus. Holy Mary, Mother of God, pray for us sinners, now and at the hour of our death. Amen.

VI.   Hail Mary, full of Grace, the Lord is with thee. Blessed art thou among women, and blessed is the fruit of thy womb, Jesus. Holy Mary, Mother of God, pray for us sinners, now and at the hour of our death. Amen.

VII.   Hail Mary, full of Grace, the Lord is with thee. Blessed art thou among women, and blessed is the fruit of thy womb, Jesus. Holy Mary, Mother of God, pray for us sinners, now and at the hour of our death. Amen.

VIII.   Hail Mary, full of Grace, the Lord is with thee. Blessed art thou among women, and blessed is the fruit of thy womb, Jesus. Holy Mary, Mother of God, pray for us sinners, now and at the hour of our death. Amen.

IX.   Hail Mary, full of Grace, the Lord is with thee. Blessed art thou among women, and blessed is the fruit of thy womb, Jesus. Holy Mary, Mother of God, pray for us sinners, now and at the hour of our death. Amen.

X.   Hail Mary, full of Grace, the Lord is with thee. Blessed art thou among women, and blessed is the fruit of thy womb, Jesus. Holy Mary, Mother of God, pray for us sinners, now and at the hour of our death. Amen.

Glory be to the Father, and to the Son, and to the Holy Spirit. As it was in the beginning, is now, and ever shall be, world without end. Amen.

O my Jesus, forgive us our sins, save us from the fires of hell, lead all souls to heaven, especially those in most need of Thy mercy. Amen.

May the Grace of this Mystery come down into my soul. Amen.

The Third Glorious Mystery;
"The Descent of the Holy Spirit"

(Spiritual Fruit; Love)

When the day of Pentecost came it found them gathered in one place. Suddenly from up in the sky there came a noise like a strong, driving wind which was heard all through the house where they were seated. (Acts 2:1-2)

Our Father, Who art in heaven, Hallowed be Thy name; Thy kingdom come; Thy will be done on earth as it is in heaven. Give us this day our daily bread; and forgive us our trespasses as we forgive those who trespass against us; and lead us not into temptation, but deliver us from evil. Amen.

I.   Hail Mary, full of Grace, the Lord is with thee. Blessed art thou among women, and blessed is the fruit of thy womb, Jesus. Holy Mary, Mother of God, pray for us sinners, now and at the hour of our death. Amen.

II.   Hail Mary, full of Grace, the Lord is with thee. Blessed art thou among women, and blessed is the fruit of thy womb, Jesus. Holy Mary, Mother of God, pray for us sinners, now and at the hour of our death. Amen.

III.   Hail Mary, full of Grace, the Lord is with thee. Blessed art thou among women, and blessed is the fruit of thy womb, Jesus. Holy Mary, Mother of God, pray for us sinners, now and at the hour of our death. Amen.

IV.   Hail Mary, full of Grace, the Lord is with thee. Blessed art thou among women, and blessed is the fruit of thy womb, Jesus. Holy Mary, Mother of God, pray for us sinners, now and at the hour of our death. Amen.

V.   Hail Mary, full of Grace, the Lord is with thee. Blessed art thou among women, and blessed is the fruit of thy womb, Jesus. Holy Mary, Mother of God, pray for us sinners, now and at the hour of our death. Amen.

VI.   Hail Mary, full of Grace, the Lord is with thee. Blessed art thou among women, and blessed is the fruit of thy womb, Jesus. Holy Mary, Mother of God, pray for us sinners, now and at the hour of our death. Amen.

VII.   Hail Mary, full of Grace, the Lord is with thee. Blessed art thou among women, and blessed is the fruit of thy womb, Jesus. Holy Mary, Mother of God, pray for us sinners, now and at the hour of our death. Amen.

VIII. Hail Mary, full of Grace, the Lord is with thee. Blessed art thou among women, and blessed is the fruit of thy womb, Jesus. Holy Mary, Mother of God, pray for us sinners, now and at the hour of our death. Amen.

IX.   Hail Mary, full of Grace, the Lord is with thee. Blessed art thou among women, and blessed is the fruit of thy womb, Jesus. Holy Mary, Mother of God, pray for us sinners, now and at the hour of our death. Amen.

X.   Hail Mary, full of Grace, the Lord is with thee. Blessed art thou among women, and blessed is the fruit of thy womb, Jesus. Holy Mary, Mother of God, pray for us sinners, now and at the hour of our death. Amen.

Glory be to the Father, and to the Son, and to the Holy Spirit. As it was in the beginning, is now, and ever shall be, world without end. Amen.

O my Jesus, forgive us our sins, save us from the fires of hell, lead all souls to heaven, especially those in most need of Thy mercy. Amen.

May the Grace of this Mystery come down into my soul. Amen.

The Fourth Glorious Mystery;
"The Assumption of Our Blessed Mother"

(Spiritual Fruit; Eternal Happiness)

But the woman was given the wings of a gigantic eagle so that she could fly off to her place in the desert, where, far from the serpent, she could be taken care of for a year and for two and a half years more. (Revelation 12:14)

Our Father, Who art in heaven, Hallowed be Thy name; Thy kingdom come; Thy will be done on earth as it is in heaven. Give us this day our daily bread; and forgive us our trespasses as we forgive those who trespass against us; and lead us not into temptation, but deliver us from evil. Amen.

I.   Hail Mary, full of Grace, the Lord is with thee. Blessed art thou among women, and blessed is the fruit of thy womb, Jesus. Holy Mary, Mother of God, pray for us sinners, now and at the hour of our death. Amen.

II. Hail Mary, full of Grace, the Lord is with thee. Blessed art thou among women, and blessed is the fruit of thy womb, Jesus. Holy Mary, Mother of God, pray for us sinners, now and at the hour of our death. Amen.

III. Hail Mary, full of Grace, the Lord is with thee. Blessed art thou among women, and blessed is the fruit of thy womb, Jesus. Holy Mary, Mother of God, pray for us sinners, now and at the hour of our death. Amen.

IV. Hail Mary, full of Grace, the Lord is with thee. Blessed art thou among women, and blessed is the fruit of thy womb, Jesus. Holy Mary, Mother of God, pray for us sinners, now and at the hour of our death. Amen.

V.   Hail Mary, full of Grace, the Lord is with thee. Blessed art thou among women, and blessed is the fruit of thy womb, Jesus. Holy Mary, Mother of God, pray for us sinners, now and at the hour of our death. Amen.

VI.   Hail Mary, full of Grace, the Lord is with thee. Blessed art thou among women, and blessed is the fruit of thy womb, Jesus. Holy Mary, Mother of God, pray for us sinners, now and at the hour of our death. Amen.

VII.   Hail Mary, full of Grace, the Lord is with thee. Blessed art thou among women, and blessed is the fruit of thy womb, Jesus. Holy Mary, Mother of God, pray for us sinners, now and at the hour of our death. Amen.

VIII.   Hail Mary, full of Grace, the Lord is with thee. Blessed art thou among women, and blessed is the fruit of thy womb, Jesus. Holy Mary, Mother of God, pray for us sinners, now and at the hour of our death. Amen.

IX.   Hail Mary, full of Grace, the Lord is with thee. Blessed art thou among women, and blessed is the fruit of thy womb, Jesus. Holy Mary, Mother of God, pray for us sinners, now and at the hour of our death. Amen.

X.   Hail Mary, full of Grace, the Lord is with thee. Blessed art thou among women, and blessed is the fruit of thy womb, Jesus. Holy Mary, Mother of God, pray for us sinners, now and at the hour of our death. Amen.

Glory be to the Father, and to the Son, and to the Holy Spirit. As it was in the beginning, is now, and ever shall be, world without end. Amen.

O my Jesus, forgive us our sins, save us from the fires of hell, lead all souls to heaven, especially those in most need of Thy mercy. Amen.

May the Grace of this Mystery come down into my soul. Amen.

The Fifth Glorious Mystery;
"The Crowning of Mary as Queen of Heaven"

(Spiritual Fruit; True Devotion to Mary)

A great portent appeared in Heaven, a woman clothed with the sun, with the moon under her feet. (Revelation 12:1)

Our Father, Who art in heaven, Hallowed be Thy name; Thy kingdom come; Thy will be done on earth as it is in heaven. Give us this day our daily bread; and forgive us our trespasses as we forgive those who trespass against us; and lead us not into temptation, but deliver us from evil. Amen.

I.   Hail Mary, full of Grace, the Lord is with thee. Blessed art thou among women, and blessed is the fruit of thy womb, Jesus. Holy Mary, Mother of God, pray for us sinners, now and at the hour of our death. Amen.

II. Hail Mary, full of Grace, the Lord is with thee. Blessed art thou among women, and blessed is the fruit of thy womb, Jesus. Holy Mary, Mother of God, pray for us sinners, now and at the hour of our death. Amen.

III. Hail Mary, full of Grace, the Lord is with thee. Blessed art thou among women, and blessed is the fruit of thy womb, Jesus. Holy Mary, Mother of God, pray for us sinners, now and at the hour of our death. Amen.

IV. Hail Mary, full of Grace, the Lord is with thee. Blessed art thou among women, and blessed is the fruit of thy womb, Jesus. Holy Mary, Mother of God, pray for us sinners, now and at the hour of our death. Amen.

V.   Hail Mary, full of Grace, the Lord is with thee. Blessed art thou among women, and blessed is the fruit of thy womb, Jesus. Holy Mary, Mother of God, pray for us sinners, now and at the hour of our death. Amen.

VI.   Hail Mary, full of Grace, the Lord is with thee. Blessed art thou among women, and blessed is the fruit of thy womb, Jesus. Holy Mary, Mother of God, pray for us sinners, now and at the hour of our death. Amen.

VII.   Hail Mary, full of Grace, the Lord is with thee. Blessed art thou among women, and blessed is the fruit of thy womb, Jesus. Holy Mary, Mother of God, pray for us sinners, now and at the hour of our death. Amen.

VIII.   Hail Mary, full of Grace, the Lord is with thee. Blessed art thou among women, and blessed is the fruit of thy womb, Jesus. Holy Mary, Mother of God, pray for us sinners, now and at the hour of our death. Amen.

IX.   Hail Mary, full of Grace, the Lord is with thee. Blessed art thou among women, and blessed is the fruit of thy womb, Jesus. Holy Mary, Mother of God, pray for us sinners, now and at the hour of our death. Amen.

X.   Hail Mary, full of Grace, the Lord is with thee. Blessed art thou among women, and blessed is the fruit of thy womb, Jesus. Holy Mary, Mother of God, pray for us sinners, now and at the hour of our death. Amen.

Glory be to the Father, and to the Son, and to the Holy Spirit. As it was in the beginning, is now, and ever shall be, world without end. Amen.

O my Jesus, forgive us our sins, save us from the fires of hell, lead all souls to heaven, especially those in most need of Thy mercy. Amen.

May the Grace of this Mystery come down into my soul. Amen.

Hail, Holy Queen, Mother of Mercy, our life, our sweetness and our hope. To you do we cry, poor banished children of Eve. To you do we send up our sighs, mourning and weeping in this valley of tears. Turn then most gracious advocate, your eyes of mercy toward us; and after this, our exile, show unto us the blessed fruit of your womb, Jesus. O clement, O loving, O sweet Virgin Mary.

V. Pray for us, O Holy Mother of God,
R. That we may be made worthy of the promises of Christ.

Let us pray. O God, whose only-begotten Son, by His life death, and resurrection, has purchased for us the rewards of eternal life, grant, we beseech Thee, that by meditating upon these Mysteries of the Most Holy Rosary of the Blessed Virgin Mary, we may imitate what they contain and obtain what they promise, through the same Christ our Lord. Amen.

My God, I believe, I adore, I hope, and I love You. I beg pardon of You for those who do not believe, do not adore, do not hope and do not love You.

St. Michael the Archangel, defend us in battle. Be our defense against the wickedness and snares of the Devil. May God rebuke him, we humbly pray, and do thou, O Prince of thy heavenly hosts, by the power of God, thrust into hell Satan and all the other evil spirits, who prowl about the world seeking the ruin of souls. Amen.

Queen of the Rosary, sweet Virgin of Fatima, who hast deigned to appear in the land of Portugal and hast brought peace, both interior and exterior, to that once so troubled country, we beg of thee to watch over our dear homeland and to assure its moral and spiritual revival.

Bring back peace to all nations of the world, so that all, and our own nation in particular, may be happy to call thee their Queen and the Queen of Peace.

Our Lady of the Rosary, pray for our country. Our Lady of Fatima, obtain for all humanity a durable peace. Amen.

In the name of the Father, and of the Son, and of the Holy Spirit. Amen.

<u>Litany of the Blessed Virgin Mary</u>

Lord, have mercy.
Christ, have mercy.
Lord, have mercy.
Christ, hear us.
Christ, graciously hear us.

God the Father of Heaven, have mercy on us.
God the Son, Redeemer of the world, have mercy on us.
God the Holy Spirit, have mercy on us.
Holy Trinity, One God, have mercy on us.

Holy Mary, pray for us.
Holy Mother of God, pray for us.
Holy Virgin of virgins, pray for us.
Mother of Christ, pray for us.
Mother of divine grace, pray for us.
Mother most pure, pray for us.
Mother most chaste, pray for us.
Mother inviolate, pray for us.
Mother undefiled, pray for us.
Mother most amiable, pray for us.
Mother most admirable, pray for us.
Mother of good counsel, pray for us.
Mother of our Creator, pray for us.
Mother of our Savior, pray for us.
Virgin most prudent, pray for us.
Virgin most venerable, pray for us.
Virgin most renowned, pray for us.
Virgin most powerful, pray for us.
Virgin most merciful, pray for us.
Virgin most faithful, pray for us.
Mirror of justice, pray for us.
Seat of wisdom, pray for us.
Cause of our joy, pray for us.
Spiritual vessel, pray for us.
Vessel of honor, pray for us.

Singular vessel of devotion, pray for us.
Mystical rose pray for us.
Tower of David, pray for us.
Tower of ivory, pray for us.
House of gold, pray for us.
Ark of the covenant, pray for us.
Gate of heaven, pray for us.
Morning star, pray for us.
Health of the sick, pray for us.
Refuge of sinners, pray for us.
Comforter of the afflicted, pray for us.
Help of Christians, pray for us.
Queen of Angels, pray for us.
Queen of Patriarchs, pray for us.
Queen of Prophets, pray for us.
Queen of Apostles, pray for us.
Queen of Martyrs, pray for us.
Queen of Confessors, pray for us.
Queen of Virgins, pray for us.
Queen of all Saints, pray for us.
Queen conceived without original sin, pray for us.
Queen assumed into heaven, pray for us.
Queen of the most Holy Rosary, pray for us.
Queen of Peace, pray for us.

Lamb of God, who takes away the sins of the world, spare us, O Lord!
Lamb of God, who takes away the sins of the world, graciously hear us,
O Lord!
Lamb of God, who takes away the sins of the world have mercy on us.

V. Pray for us, O Holy Mother of God.
R. That we may be made worthy of the promises of Christ.

Let us pray. Grant we beseech Thee, O Lord God, that
we Thy servants, may enjoy perpetual health of mind
and body; and, by the glorious intercession of the Blessed
Mary, Ever Virgin, be delivered from present sorrow and
obtain eternal joy. Through Christ, our Lord. Amen.

Memorare of St. Bernard

Remember, O most gracious Virgin Mary, that never was it known that anyone who fled to your protection, implored your help or sought your intercession was left unaided.

Inspired by this confidence, I fly unto thee, O Virgin of virgins, my mother, to thee do I come, before thee I stand, sinful and sorrowful. O Mother of the Word Incarnate, despise not my petitions, but in your mercy hear and answer me. Amen.

(For the intentions of the Holy Father, one may recite at the end of the Rosary one "Our Father", one "Hail Mary", and one "Glory Be")

Mother Mary, a Term of Royalty!
Mary is the New Eve!
Woman!

The Fifteen Promises of Mary to Christians
Who Recite the Rosary

(Given to St. Dominic and Blessed Alan)

1. Whoever shall faithfully serve me by the recitation of the Rosary, shall receive signal graces.

2. I promise my special protection and the greatest graces to all those who shall recite the Rosary.

3. The Rosary shall be a powerful armor against hell, it will destroy vice, decrease sin and defeat heresies.

4. It will cause virtues and good works to flourish; it will obtain for souls the abundant mercy of God; it will withdraw the hearts of men from the love of the world and its vanities and will lift them to the desire of eternal things. Oh, that souls would sanctify themselves by this means.

5. The soul which recommends itself to me by the recitation of the Rosary shall not perish.

6. Whoever shall recite the Rosary devoutly, applying himself to the consideration of its Sacred Mysteries shall never be conquered by misfortune. God will not chastise him in His justice; he shall not perish by an unprovided death; if he be just, he shall remain in the grace of God and become worthy of eternal life.

7. Whoever shall have a true devotion for the Rosary shall not die without the Sacraments of the Church.

8. Those who are faithful to recite the Rosary shall have during their life and at their death the light of God and the plentitude of His graces; at the moment of death they shall participate in the merits of the Saints in Paradise.

9. I shall deliver from Purgatory those who have been devoted to the Rosary.

10. The faithful children of the Rosary shall merit a high degree of glory in heaven.

11. You shall obtain all you ask of me by the recitation of the Rosary.

12. All those who propagate the Holy Rosary shall be aided by me in their necessities.

13. I have obtained from my Divine Son that all the advocates of the Rosary shall have intercessors, the entire celestial court, during their life and at the hour of death.

14. All who recite the Rosary are my sons, and brothers of my only Son, Jesus Christ.

15. Devotion to my Rosary is a great sign of predestination.

Words of Our Lady of Fatima on the Holy Rosary

May 13, 1917, Pray the Rosary every day, in order to obtain peace for the world, and the end of the war.

June 13, 1917, I wish you to come here on the 13th of next month to pray the Rosary each day.

July 13, 1917, I want you to come here on the 13th of next month, and to continue praying the Rosary every day in honor of Our Lady of the Rosary, in order to obtain peace for the world and the end of the war, because only She can help you.

August 19, 1917, I want you to continue praying the Rosary every day.

September 13, 1917, continue to say the Rosary to obtain the end of the war.

October 13, 1917, I am Our Lady of the Rosary. Continue to say the Rosary every day.

December 10, 1925, (to Sister Lucia at Monteverdi) You at least try to console Me and announce in My name that I promise to assist at the moment of death, with all the graces necessary for salvation, all those who on the First Saturday of five consecutive months shall confess, receive Holy Communion, recite five decades of the Rosary, and keep Me company for fifteen minutes while meditating on the *fifteen Mysteries of the Rosary,* with the intention of making Reparation to Me.

The Twelve Promises of the Sacred Heart

(As given by our Lord to Saint Margaret Mary Alacoque)

1. I will give them all the graces necessary for their state of life.

2. I will give peace in their families.

3. I will console them in all their troubles.

4. They shall find in My Heart an assure refuge during life and especially the hour of death.

5. I will pour out abundant blessings on all their undertakings.

6. Sinners shall find in My Heart the source and infinite ocean of mercy.

7. Tepid souls shall become fervent.

8. Fervent souls shall speedily rise to great perfection.

9. I will bless the homes in which the image of My Sacred Heart shall be exposed and honored.

10. I will give to priests the power to touch the most hardened hearts.

11. Those who propagate this devotion shall have their name written in My Heart, and it shall never be effaced.

12. The all-powerful love of My Heart will grant to those who shall receive Communion on the First Friday of nine consecutive months the grace of final repentance; they shall not die under My displeasure, nor without receiving their Sacraments; My Heart shall be their assured refuge at the last hour.

<u>Anima Christi</u>

Soul of Christ, make me holy. Body of Christ, save me. Blood of Christ, fill me with love. Water from Christ's side, wash me. Passion of Christ, strengthen me. Good Jesus, hear me. Within Your wounds, hide me. Never let me be parted from You. From the evil enemy, protect me. At the hour of my death, call me. And tell me to come to You. That with Your saints I may praise You. Through all eternity. Amen.

RANDOM POETRY & SONGS...

"Holy Spirit In The Holy Water"

Holy Spirit on the Holy Water,
Please cleanse me! Please cleanse me!

Holy Spirit in the Holy Water,
Please guard me! Please guard me!

REPEAT & FADE

"Gabriel, Ring The Bell"

Ch ch cha! Ch ch cha!

Gabriel,
Ring the bell!
Let there be Shalom for Noel!

Shalom on earth!
Praise be our Savior's birth!
Imagine what that is worth!

Ch ch cha! Ch ch cha! Ch ch cha!

Shalom, Shalom, Shalom, Shalom,Shalom, Shalom!
Shalom, Shalom, Shalom, Shalom,Shalom, Shalom!

Gabriel,
Ring the bell!
Let there be Shalom for Noel!

Shalom on earth!
Praise be our Savior's birth!
Imagine what that is worth!

Ch ch cha! Ch ch cha!

Shalom, Shalom, Shalom, Shalom, Shalom, Shalom!
Shalom, Shalom, Shalom, Shalom, Shalom, Shalom!

Ch ch cha! Ch ch cha! Ch ch cha!

Imagine what that is worth!!!

"Honk if You Love Jesus"

Honk if you love Jesus!
Honk if you can promise!
Honk if you attend His Service!

Honk...Honk... Honk...Real loud!
Honk...Honk...Honk...For the crowd!
Honk...Honk...Honk...Make the Lord proud!

If your honk can handle Jesus!
Then you can get through your crisis!
You will know that you're precious!

Honk if you love Jesus!
Honk if you can promise!
Honk if you attend His Service!

Honk...Honk... Honk...Real loud!
Honk...Honk...Honk...For the crowd!
Honk...Honk...Honk...Make the Lord proud!

If your honk can handle Jesus!
Then you can get through your crisis!
You will know that you're precious!

Honk! Honk! Honk! For Jesus!

"The Last Out"

Top of the 9th, with 2 outs, the score's 3-2,
Gunderson's in and he knows what to do...

The Championship's on the line,
So much is going through his mind...

You got one on 1st and one on 3rd,
Throw strikes and out's the word...

Instead, batter hits, it's a pop fly,
Graham in centerfield makes the catch, we all could cry...

The game is over we have won,
Celebrations have just begun...

Coach Casey's son runs down to join the jubilation,
Dog pile & coolers poured, Omaha becomes Beaver Nation...

As the officials give Coach Casey the award,
He thanks his family, the teams & the Lord...

Gunderson breaks a record in this saving game,
The team makes history and will never be the same...

With an '06 NCAA Baseball title in hand,
Oregon State University is great land!

"Super Moon Dancer"

Soakin' up the lunar light,
Walkin' at midnight,
Watchin' the stoplights!

Not sayin' much,
Feelin' your touch!
In love with this Dutch!

The city soundin' sweet,
Somethin' in its beat!
Just had a bite to eat!

On cue, 5th Avenue, lookin' cool,
Sergeant Sanders, meanders, by dancers,
The super moon made you bust a move,
Making you a moon-dancer, romancer, my answer!
The super moon made you bust a move!

Movin' to the rhythm of the night,
What a beautiful sight!
My Marine, holdin' me tight!

It was like magic,
So dynamic,
Lookin' photographic!

Makin' me smile,
Always loyal,
Must have walked a mile!

On cue, 5th Avenue, lookin' cool,
Sergeant Sanders, meanders, by dancers,
The super moon made you bust a move,
Making you a moon-dancer, romancer, my answer!
The super moon made you bust a move!

Lunar light, midnight, stoplight, holdin' me tight!
Always loyal, makin' me smile, walkin' a mile.
Like magic, dynamic, photographic!
The super moon made you bust a move!

On cue, 5th Avenue, lookin' cool,
Sergeant Sanders, meanders, by dancers,
The super moon made you bust a move,
Making you a moon-dancer, romancer, my answer!
The super moon made you bust a move!

The super moon made you bust a move!
Super moon dancer...
Super moon dancer...
My answer!

Ya!

"Forever Friends"

Oh how..

I'm missin' his daily love & laughter,
Trying to keep his sense of humor!

I am missing my Forever Friend,
I will love him until my end!

Forever Friends are forever,
That 's just what we are...
That's why we were together!

The things we laughed at, nobody got,
Laughter is what we caught!

He may not walk this earth in physical,
I feel him daily, it's mystical!

Forever Friends are forever,
That 's just what we are...
That's why we were together!

Teddy bear picnic's for grownups
Were coffee & muffins at sun up!

Sunrises and sunsets,
Friendship & love gifts!

Forever Friends are forever,
That 's just what we are...
That's why we were together!

The laughter and love none can compare,
We were happy at home, going nowhere!

Forever Friends are forever, forever, forever!

"Pilot"

She said, "I'm afraid of falling",
And he whispered, "I have wings,
Don't be afraid of anything"...

Because I was born to fly, fly, fly...fly with you!
Fly the plane, fly the plane, I'll fly the plane!

Flying lessons for take-off,
You can Co-Pilot the Aircraft,
On the jumbo jetliner,
Let the wind lift us up, smile and laugh!

With clouds in the Sky,
Or a bright sunny day!
Remember your Pilot is with you all the way!

Because I was born to fly, fly, fly...fly with you!
Fly the plane, fly the plane, I'll fly the plane!

The engine is the heart of the plane,
But the Pilot is its soul,
Which I'll remain!

Oh Co-Pilot, where do you want to go?
Don't be afraid,
We'll fly over & under the rainbows!

Time flies and I'm your Pilot,
I have wings,
Don't be afraid of falling,
Or anything!
A direct flight,
Is in sight!

Fly the plane, fly the plane, I'll fly the plane, I'm your Pilot, I was born
to fly, fly, fly...fly with you!
I was born to fly, fly, fly...
Fly with you!

"Love All Day"

Daffodils and tulips,
Peonies & bees!
Koi fish,
Casserole dish,
A pot of tea!

Grandfather clock,
Playing tic toc!
Front porch cover!
Dutch lights,
Fill the nights,
You're my lover!

Singing from the keyboard,
At home with you!
China in the cupboard,
Feeling brand new!

Donuts for breakfast,
Cadillac to drive!
Monet necklace,
Baby, I'm alive!

Loving Mother,
Old Glory in her pride!
Calling our brother,
A Marine flag beside!

Company to visit,
Flowers in prime!
Pleasant just to sit,
Sauna time!

Pretty Artwork,
To empower!
Coffee ready to perk,
Always Happy hour!

Occasional champagne,
Laughter and meals!
A little weight gain,
Stock market deals!

Light the fire,
Rhyming words!
As we tire,
Watching the birds!

Fresh bouquets,
A creek in the floor!
Love all day,
Who could ask for anything more?...
Who could ask?...
Who could ask?...
Who could ask?...For anything mooooooorrrreeee!

"Spring"

It's Spring take off the bling, just sing and dance!
It's time for new romance!

Looking good, in the hood, I'm in the mood to dance, It's time for new romance!

No holding back,
I don't lack!
Kick up your heels,
We'll have some meals!
Get your wheels a dancin',
It's time for new romancin'!

The band is playin',
I'm just sayin'!

And if the music's a hit,
Never miss a chance to dance!
When the music's playing, don't sit!

Dance to you own beat,
Just move your feet!

Hip hop, social dancin',
It's time for new romancin'!

It's Spring, take off the bling, just sing and dance!
It's time for new romance.

Dance...It's time for new romance!

"Divine Love Song"

Early birds and night owls,
It's a personal invitation,
For a major eye candy sugar high!
When young is helping old,
When there is love among all,
When our Divine songs sing together,

When we live in peace!

Something so magical,
As...
In the beginning where there was,
Divine Love...
Who created the heavens and the earth...
Who now lives in each of us!
Who now lives through each of us!
Who now lives amongst each of us!
Who now lives to give life to us!

What kind of life are you looking for?
Do you adore?
Will you show for sure?
Will you implore?

Simply sparkle, find your treasure,
Is it leisure or adventure,
Something only you can measure!

Come & dine!
Then shimmer in the fine,
Spotlight of your design!
Align and shine,
Where love is Divine!

Sent from above, fits like a glove,
Of Divine Love,
Who created the heavens and the earth...
Who now lives in each of us!
Who now lives through each of us!
Who now lives amongst each of us!
Who now lives to give life to us!

Doll it's a treasure worth finding available to all...
A call a cure all, a windfall like a waterfall!
It never dies, it's for all the shy & the wise!

Divine Love...
Who created the heavens and the earth...
Who now lives in each of us!
Who now lives through each of us!
Who now lives amongst each of us!
Who now lives to give life to us!

Divine Love never dies,
It's for all the shy & the wise!
Personal invitation to,
Divine Love...
Divine Love...
Divine Love!

"Billy Joel's My Dream"

Images of you Billy Joel in my head,
Dreamin' of being your newlywed!
Will you play, just for me?
I will dance & listen hourly!
I will make your favorite food...Invite friends from the hood!

La la la di da da
La la di di da da dum!

Billy Joel, my dream is,
Someday, to marry you!
I'll be your back up, collaborator, lover!
Let's build a future! Take me to the altar!
The Piano Man and Lee Ann,
Let's plan to begin in Branson!

Bring out all the instruments you can find...Your buddies will play along, unwind!
1,2,3 from the drummer...We will kick off summer!

La la la di da da
La la di di da da dum!

Billy Joel, my dream is,
Someday, to marry you!
I'll be your backup, collaborator, lover!
Let's build a future! Take me to the altar!
The Piano Man and Lee Ann,
Let's plan to begin in Branson!

Billy Joel, you're my dream, my future, my someday!
My someday!
Someday!
Oh to be your lover! At the altar!
With you, we'd build a future!
I need the Piano Man, with whom I'd begin!

La la la di da da
La la di di da da dum!

Billy Joel, my dream is,
Someday, to marry you!
I'll be your backup, collaborator, lover!
Let's build a future! Take me to the altar!
The Piano Man and Lee Ann,
Let's plan to begin in Branson!

"Made Out of Junk"

In each piece, there's a memory for sure,
In my jewelry Christmas tree picture!
It glistens, it shines, it catches attention,
Oh, by the way, did I happen to mention?
As I look at it up on the wall,
I vividly remember them all!

Let's start at the top with the shining star,

This one is certainly my fave by far!

The crown my Mother bought one like,
Reminds me of the Prince of Life!

I lost some earrings, so they fill in the spaces,
Between where I have been, all of the nice places!

The roses bring me back to the garden I had,
Where I would cut all the flowers, even the bad!

In each piece, there's a memory for sure,
In my jewelry Christmas tree picture!
It glistens, it shines, it catches attention,
Oh, by the way, did I happen to mention?
As I look at it up on the wall,
I vividly remember them all!

The golden pear pin reminds me of my sister,
She had a brooch collection, oh how I miss her!

The spider like cone brings memories of Grandpa,
He didn't like spiders, of him, I was in awe!

The big brooch right in the middle had earrings to match,
In business I wore them a lot, where I would dispatch!

The big circling bling on the bottom,
I would start wearing in the Autumn.

In each piece, there's a memory for sure,
In my jewelry Christmas tree picture!
It glistens, it shines, it catches attention,
Oh, by the way, did I happen to mention?
As I look at it up on the wall,
I vividly remember them all!

The pearls, you know, are always the great classics,
I've been many places, but not the arctics!

I sent for more jewels from the internet,
Lookin' good just like my cousin Annette!

Some of these sweet honey's may be a little old lady,
When I needed to wear them they were eternally ready!

I always wanted to wear the lovely bow,
But for some strange reason, it just didn't go!

In each piece, there's a memory for sure,
In my jewelry Christmas tree picture!
It glistens, it shines, it catches attention,
Oh, by the way, did I happen to mention?
As I look at it up on the wall,
I vividly remember them all!

The squares at the bottom strongly represent the trunk,
All this jewelry tells a story, made out of junk!

A memory for sure, a picture,
That catches attention, I mention,
The wall, where I remember them all...
From the top of the star to the bottom trunk,
A story made out of junk...Made out of junk!

"That Boy"

Great-Grandma Mary named him, "That Boy"!
Like a new toy....
He brought her great joy?

He took her breath away...
The first day...
He came to play!

So many great-grandchildren...
Came before him...
Like the others, her heart he'd win!

Her memory was slippin'...
But not her love of Ryan...
Seeing him she was smilin'!

I think back to the day he was born...
We came to adorn...
His face was crooked, but no scorn!

The doctor said...
The baby's head...
Was twisted in the womb bed!

Give it a few weeks...
He'll have the right cheeks...
No need to be weak!

That Boy, was off and could run...
Handsome child from day one...
Somehow, he loved to hunt!

Too bad Great-Grandpa Archie & Grandpa Richard passed on...
While he was quite young...
They could have hunted together, at the rising sun!

But Uncle Sam would teach him to fish...
His Dad would BBQ a salmon dish...
His bucket list, shooting an elk, he would wish!

With three down, in the past five years...
His friends couldn't believe their ears...
Happy to mount any deers!

College grad...
And so glad...

Needed to get a job bad!

Working in construction now...
Woodburn's where he started out...
Just like the garbage route!

Always wanted to serve in the military...
Grandma Arvella speaks of Grandpa Tom's legacy...
Not in the cards as of yet, though we'll see!

That Boy enjoys basketball, sideline court...
Baseball is his favorite sport...
Meeting cousins & friends at the golf course!

Up for any OSU football game...
Even if it's in the rain...
Lifting weights, muscles to gain!

Someday to have land...
On a farm or near the sand...
Even over looking meadowland!

That Boy, made a fine ring bearer once...
He will make a great husband...
His life will always be fun!

A future so bright...
You can see his light...
Like a flying kite!

Always happy and looking fit...
Just the right wit...
That Boy is it!

A fine brother & uncle, Anthony's his buddy, like Al...
Love of any animal...
Probably could have been musical!

Grandmother's proud as she can be...
Bragging on him are his Auntie's....
Sally, Kay, Mary, Joan, Molly, Loreen, Marie and Me!

His Mother is a given...
She loves him to no end...
And there when he would first begin!

Love to Eternity, my blessed Nephew...
May God's favor and blessings always carry you...
Recognizing Him walking at your side too!

Need I say..?
I love you, all the way...LA
P.S...
Guess..?
We're getting turf not grass!!!

"Dear Niece"

"Hello Beautiful!"
May these words seem musical!

I want to wish you a Happy Birthday!
A few things I'd like to say...

Thank you for all the joy you have brought me,
It's easy for you to bring glee!

Wow has it been really been 39 years...
Pondering time brings me to tears.

It was yesterday, right...
That I held you Baby tight...

I always wanted to babysit you,
It was so much fun all night through!

You loved to stay up late, sleep I wanted,
It was in that time that we bonded!

For some reason your hair wouldn't grow,
But when it decided to, beauty it showed!

You and Jack would come over,
Now you're like Crimson & Clover!

I must say you are looking pretty,
Often funny & very witty!

I know you are turning 39 dear Niece,
But it's your #1 birth right, of which I speak!

Yes, you are number one forever,
Happy Birthday Eve Shawna, I'm glad we're together!

I love you to Eternity,
Always & evermore, LA, your Auntie!

"Happy Birthday Lori Ann"

Happy Birthday Lori Ann,
Hope it's the greatest in all the land!

Feel the love for you,
All day through!

Make your wish,
For all that's bliss!

Time with your boys & Ken,
Be sure to take it all in!

Enjoy your new year,
You are a lovely dear!

Glad you are my sis,
Seeing you I miss!

Birthday hugs & kisses all day long,
I'll be singing your Birthday song!

Lovey dove!

"Hey Dear Friend"

Hey Dear Friend
I love you!
There's no doubt,
Things are working out!

Some have walked in your shoes
Still rebound, You will too!

Never, never give up!

It's a climb, one step at a time,
Yesterday's history,
Tomorrow's a mystery!
Today is a gift!
Giving you a lift!

Some think they have no value,
But this is the truth,
When given new chance,
Go on to greatness.

Never, never give up!

It's a climb, one step at a time,
Yesterday's history,
Tomorrow's a mystery!
Today is a gift!

Giving you a lift!

Write a book tell your story!
Give thanks, praise & glory!

You are going to do great things,
Bring your offerings.
Keep going!
New life is showing!

Love & appreciation,
Wisdom and determination!
Always choose kindness,
And forgiveness!

Never, never give up!

It's a climb, one step at a time,
Yesterday is history,
Tomorrow's a mystery!
Today is a gift!
Giving you a lift!

Creativity leads to prosperity!

Never, never give up!
Never, never give up!

"What You're Living For"

What do you want from me Lord? That's the question...
How will I know it is you? Did I happen to mention?

I don't like pain, change will do.
Lead me on a new path all the way through!

Will you be providing my supplies?

My husbands gone now, wipe the tears from my eyes.

My love for him made me strong,
It's time to write a new song!

With a sense of courage,
May I turn the page?

How do I take the first step?
Getting quiet to check.

In the silence I will hear.
Your words to me, I hold so dear.

Seems you say, "Just wait, not yet!
Stay the course and do not jet!

I will be getting back to you,
It's too early to tell you what to do!

For now get your work done and smile more!
Happiness is what you're living for!"

"S&H Greenstamps"

It was S&H Greenstamps, where I got my start,
My Mother traded, so I could begin my art!

Inspired by girls at camp who new some chords,
I've written my own songs in my own words!

Dedicated a special song to my beautiful Mother,
Because she was like no other!

Playing and jamming at weddings for any loved one,
Gave me a stage to shine under the sun!

My goal is to get my music to the masses,
I am self taught, not in classes!

The time is now, to get my music published,
It's a lifelong goal of what I've always wished!

So I may be the first to thank S&H Greenstamps,
My Mother's seed planted long ago, so I could learn amps!

My guitar is truly a friend,
My mission is to entertain to the end!!!

"You Saved Me"

Love, you saved me,
I couldn't go another year,
Not being myself.
Love, you saved me,
I'm not like all the rest.

Something deep inside told me just to be,
Even though I thought I had to be someone else.
I painted up & went along with the crowd,
Just so I didn't stand out.
I was to never show my tears.

Then I met Love.
You influenced me to just be myself.

Love, you saved me.
I couldn't go another year,
of not being myself.
Love, you saved me,
I'm not like all the rest.

I figured it out and I can't be held back anymore.
Now life's victorious, I don't have to be anyone else.

With confidence I grew back to being myself.
Such a favor, you gave me Love!

Then I met Love.
You influenced me to just be myself.
Love, you saved me!

Being myself, it's the best thing to be,
Breaking free baby.

Love, you saved me.

"A Ditty..."

Go cancer, be gone...
Go cancer, be gone...
Go cancer, be gone..

Be gone forever!

In the name of the Father, and of the Son, and of the Holy Spirit. Amen.

Keep Praying...Keep Praying...Keep Praying...Keep Praying...Keep Praying...
Keep Praying...Keep Praying...Keep Praying...Keep Praying...Keep Praying...
Keep Praying...Keep Praying...Keep Praying...Keep Praying...Keep Praying...
Keep Praying...Keep Praying...Keep Praying...Keep Praying...Keep Praying...
Keep Praying...Keep Praying...Keep Praying...Keep Praying...Keep Praying...
Keep Praying...Keep Praying...Keep Praying...Keep Praying...Keep Praying...
Keep Praying...Keep Praying...Keep Praying...Keep Praying...Keep Praying...
Keep Praying...Keep Praying...Keep Praying...Keep Praying...Keep Praying...
Keep Praying...Keep Praying...Keep Praying...Keep Praying...Keep Praying...
Keep Praying...Keep Praying...Keep Praying...Keep Praying...Keep Praying...
Keep Praying...Keep Praying...Keep Praying...Keep Praying...Keep Praying...
Keep Praying...Keep Praying...Keep Praying...Keep Praying...Keep Praying...
Keep Praying...Keep Praying...Keep Praying...Keep Praying...Keep Praying...
Keep Praying...Keep Praying...Keep Praying...Keep Praying...Keep Praying...
Keep Praying...Keep Praying...Keep Praying...Keep Praying...Keep Praying...
Keep Praying...Keep Praying...Keep Praying...Keep Praying...Keep Praying...
Keep Praying...Keep Praying...Keep Praying...Keep Praying...Keep Praying...
Keep Praying...Keep Praying...Keep Praying...Keep Praying...Keep Praying...
Keep Praying...Keep Praying...Keep Praying...Keep Praying...Keep Praying...
Keep Praying...Keep Praying...Keep Praying...Keep Praying...Keep Praying...
Keep Praying...Keep Praying...Keep Praying...Keep Praying...Keep Praying...
Keep Praying...Keep Praying...Keep Praying...Keep Praying...Keep Praying...
Keep Praying...Keep Praying...Keep Praying...Keep Praying...Keep Praying...
Keep Praying...Keep Praying...Keep Praying...Keep Praying...Keep Praying...
Keep Praying...Keep Praying...Keep Praying...Keep Praying...Keep Praying...
Keep Praying...Keep Praying...Keep Praying...Keep Praying...Keep Praying...
Keep Praying...Keep Praying...Keep Praying...Keep Praying...Keep Praying...
Keep Praying...Keep Praying...Keep Praying...Keep Praying...Keep Praying...
Keep Praying...Keep Praying...Keep Praying...Keep Praying...Keep Praying...
Keep Praying...Keep Praying...Keep Praying...Keep Praying...Keep Praying...
Keep Praying...Keep Praying...Keep Praying...Keep Praying...Keep Praying...
Keep Praying...Keep Praying...Keep Praying...Keep Praying...Keep Praying...
Keep Praying...Keep Praying...Keep Praying...Keep Praying...Keep Praying...
Keep Praying...Keep Praying...Keep Praying...Keep Praying...Keep Praying...
Keep Praying...Keep Praying...Keep Praying...Keep Praying...Keep Praying...
Keep Praying...Keep Praying...Keep Praying...Keep Praying...Keep Praying...
Keep Praying...Keep Praying...Keep Praying...Keep Praying...Keep Praying...
Keep Praying...Keep Praying...Keep Praying...Keep Praying...Keep Praying...